Praise for *Too You...*

© Marika and Howard Stone

Marika and Howard Stone are cofounders of 2young2retire.com, an online community of retirement alternatives. Howard enjoyed a long career in international advertising sales and magazine publishing before he became a certified life coach at age sixty-four. Marika is the editorial director of 2young2retire.com and has been a journalist, English teacher, public relations account executive, and small-businesss owner. She is also a certified Kripalu yoga teacher. The Stones live in Rhode Island.

Too Young to Retire

101 Ways to Start
the Rest of Your Life

Marika and Howard Stone

A PLUME BOOK

PLUME
Published by the Penguin Group
Penguin Group (USA) Inc., 375 Hudson Street, New York, New York 10014, U.S.A.
Penguin Books Ltd, 80 Strand, London WC2R 0RL, England
Penguin Books Australia Ltd, 250 Camberwell Road, Camberwell, Victoria 3124, Australia
Penguin Books Canada Ltd, 10 Alcorn Avenue, Toronto, Ontario, Canada M4V 3B2
Penguin Books India (P) Ltd, 11 Community Centre, Panchsheel Park, New Delhi–110 017, India
Penguin Books (N.Z.) Ltd, Cnr Rosedale and Airborne Roads, Albany, Auckland 1310, New Zealand
Penguin Books (South Africa) (Pty) Ltd, 24 Sturdee Avenue, Rosebank, Johannesburg 2196, South Africa

Penguin Books Ltd, Registered Offices: 80 Strand, London WC2R 0RL, England

First published by Plume, a member of Penguin Group (USA) Inc.

First Printing, May 2004
10   9   8   7   6   5   4   3   2   1

2young2retire is a registered trademark of 2young2retire Media LLC.

REGISTERED TRADEMARK—MARCA REGISTRADA

CIP data is available.
ISBN 0-452-28557-7

Printed in the United States of America
Set in Vendetta Light with Base 9   Designed by Daniel Lagin

PUBLISHER'S NOTE
While the author has made every effort to provide accurate telephone numbers and Internet addresses at the time of publication, neither the publisher nor the author assumes any responsibility for errors, or for changes that occur after publication.

The scanning, uploading, and distribution of this book via the Internet or via any other means without the permission of the publisher is illegal and punishable by law. Please purchase only authorized electronic editions, and do not participate in or encourage electronic piracy of copyrighted materials. Your support of the authors' rights is appreciated.

BOOKS ARE AVAILABLE AT QUANTITY DISCOUNTS WHEN USED TO PROMOTE PRODUCTS OR SERVICES. FOR INFORMATION PLEASE WRITE TO PREMIUM MARKETING DIVISION, PENGUIN GROUP (USA) INC., 375 HUDSON STREET, NEW YORK, NEW YORK 10014.

This book is dedicated to our children and grandchildren,
the ageless adventurers of the future.

Table of Contents

Acknowledgments

Thanks to the many ageless adventurers who contributed their stories to www.2young2retire.com, The Web Site of Retirement Alternatives, and to this work. Without their encouragement, generosity, and willingness to share details of their journey into the uncharted and as yet unnamed post-career phase of life (formerly known as retirement), we might not have been inspired and challenged to look beyond the status quo.

We also wish to express gratitude to our editor, Julia Hough, whose fine-tuning, sensitivity to the subject, and generosity of spirit were invaluable, and to our designer, Joan Harmon, whose Big Eye is equaled by her big heart.

Too Young to Retire

Introduction

The rest of your life is uncharted territory, full of twists, switchbacks, surprises, and bumps. Not so different from life so far, come to think of it. Retirement, the longed-for goal of a previous generation, is irrelevant for you, the inhabitant of a new century, with different—and evolving—models for work, play, relationships, and a meaningful life. The truth is, retirement is a social experiment that has outlived its promise, if it ever fulfilled it in the first place. When Social Security was created in 1935, few lived long enough to enjoy their so-called golden age.

You can expect not only to live longer than previous generations (a bonus of twenty or thirty years according to the latest research), but to enjoy good health for more of those years. You can look ahead to choices inconceivable to your parents and grandparents— opportunities they could barely dream of. The one-size-fits-all formulas that served as retirement planning in their day are inadequate in ours. Life is too long for a single-minded pursuit of safety and material comforts.

Consider this book an off-the-road map to the rest of your life. It is about discovery, surprise, and blazing your own trail. It isn't about destinations; it's about the journey itself. We will introduce you to other adventurers who are living the rest of their lives *their* way. These adventurers have demolished the stereotypes of what it meant to be fifty, sixty, or even ninety, doing what they could, with what they had, right where they were, as Theodore Roosevelt advised. Use this book to let yourself wander . . . and wonder.

The Story of Us

What made us, a "preretiree" couple with two incomes, a steadily appreciating home, children gone, and last pet dearly departed, opt out of a Sunbelt retirement? Why have we launched a Web site advocating the same for others?

The short answer:

You've heard of a near-death experience—the tunnel, the glowing light, the deceased loved ones, and then *wham*! You wake up at the accident scene and nothing about your life will ever be the same. Ours was a near-fatal brush with retirement, from which we awoke with an unexpected mission to share what we learned.

The longer answer:

About a dozen years ago, we attended a National Association of Food Equipment Manufacturers seminar in Palm Springs, California. Howard, then fifty-five, was founder/publisher of an annual directory for the food-service industry, the perfect grace note to a long career in advertising sales. Marika, forty-nine, was along for the ride, taking an R&R break from her work as a freelance business writer.

To so-called retirement planners, we must have seemed the perfect candidates for their services. Our two incomes supported a pleasant lifestyle and with college bills easing, we had begun to save and invest a larger percentage of our income. Retirement was in the back of our minds, like a dull headache, except occasionally in the middle of the night, Marika—financial newsletter junkie that she was—would startle awake with the thought, "Omigod! We don't have nearly enough money saved to generate the 70 percent of our current income all the experts told us was required for a comfortable existence." Discovering Palm Springs calmed those middle-of-the-night panic attacks. Rattling around in our five-bedroom New Jersey home, we had already given some thought to downsizing. Housing in California was affordable; in fact, local real estate values were perhaps at their lowest point in decades. The desert climate was ideal for a couple that loved the outdoors. We estimated that, with a little catch-up effort, our savings and investments would be more than enough to finance a comfortable retirement.

The universe must have been eavesdropping because a direct-sale opportunity came our way less than six months later, and we acted on it. An adobe condo with glorious mountain views, nearby pool, tennis courts, and hiking trails became our second home, a place for long winter breaks, a test-drive of the retirement life we imagined we wanted. After all, didn't everyone?

But a funny thing happened on the way to our "golden years." The more we experienced the lifestyle and community, the less certain we were that our decision was the right one for us. Over the course of ten winters, we spent at least six and sometimes as many as ten weeks at a time in Palm Springs, setting up temporary shop there. Nearby LAX enabled Howard to make frequent business trips to Asia and elsewhere. A computer, printer, and fax were all Marika needed to serve her clients, including some she never met face to face.

But if anything troubled our sleep, it was the prospect of our second, getaway home turning into a permanent residence. Could we idle away the hours making small talk, puttering around the garden, decorating or redecorating our condo, and waiting for visits from our (yet unborn) grandchildren to break the tedium of a life that was without direction or purpose? Could we, with our thousands of hours between us in personal-development workshops, settle for that? Much of what we noticed about retirement called to mind Dave Barry's quip about the fine line between hobbies and mental illness. We also began to see the correlation between too much time on your hands and obsessive concerns about money, possessions, and failing health.

Had this been a work of fiction, you might have expected an earthshaking "Hell no, we won't go!" but real life isn't usually like that. So, what eventually led us to conclude that, as was once said of New York City, retirement was a great place to visit, but who in their right mind would want to live there? In the quiet of many a Palm Springs evening, we found the time to read, think, and talk about where we were and where we appeared to be headed. We were absorbing stacks of material on retirement and aging "issues," noticing to our dismay the persistent view of retirement as an entitlement, something one "earned" and inevitable for everyone. To judge from most of this, the only questions worth considering were "when" you were ready and how you would pay for a life of leisure.

There were some dissenting voices, too. These include Betty Friedan's *The Fountain of Age*[1] (1993) and Theodore Roszak's *America the Wise: The Longevity Revolution and the True Wealth of Nations* (1998), both by authors in late middle age, and prime examples of the "New People," Roszak's term for members of a new, yet to be named movement of "the most adventurous, assertive, astute senior generation we have known." We were also stirred by Marc Freedman's *Prime Time: How Baby Boomers Will Revolutionize Retirement and Transform America* (1999), a passionate argument for addressing societal problems with the "windfall" of mature, experienced volunteers.

1. See Resources for more information about this and other works cited throughout the text.

Friedan, best known for her groundbreaking work in freeing millions of women from the prison of the feminine mystique, here nails the equally devastating "mystique of age." "The important consideration," she writes, "may not be, is there life after work, but how might work, freed from the drives for power and success that have dominated men (and now women) through midlife, serve the evolving needs of human life in these new years of age?" Amen.

Historian Roszak, famous for his book, *The Making of a Counterculture*, sees the potential of enormous good from the imminent "generation of senior dominance." We have the choice of providing leadership in a great task that unites us across the generations, he writes, to embrace our "first order of responsibility . . . to secure justice and make life fulfilling." Because of our numbers, the values we live by "cannot help but be a commanding influence in shaping the century to come."

Few people in the financial community, advertising, or the popular media are paying serious attention to the human (social and economic) potential in the most important demographic change in modern history. But for us, these were words to live by. They fed our longing for work that would let us stretch, grow, and be of service while making a modest income. Work we could do in some form for the rest of our lives.

Retiring Retirement

Despite the persistence of financial formulas based on conventional assumptions found in mass-market magazines like *Money*, *Worth*, and *Kiplinger's*, we have noticed a shift in the public dialogue about retirement. Even the AARP, whose first act of disassociation was to drop its full name—American Association of Retired Persons—sounds ready to retire retirement. We would like to think that www.2young2retire.com played some small part in hastening the demise of this dated concept. The truth is, we had no trouble collecting stories for 2young2retire from vital, energetic fifty-, sixty- and seventy-somethings who were anything *but* retired. Liberated, perhaps, from longtime careers they hadn't always liked, for work that was also personally fulfilling, meaningful, even fun, and that produced an income. We began to see in these "early adopters," a taste for risk taking once considered the exclusive domain of much younger folks. A professor emeritus was motivated to launch his postponed acting career. Two attorneys closed their high-pressure law practices and bought and transformed a historic inn into a successful business. A former naval officer launched a non-profit dedicated to saving street children. An engineer established a nonprofit organization dedicated to saving the earth . . . well, you get the idea.

Experts like author/gerontologist/psychologist Ken Dychtwald, Ph.D. (a wearer of many hats himself), point out that the three-stage cycle of human development—education, work, and retirement—is under revision and may disappear. More of us, he believes, will mix and match at will, taking sabbaticals throughout life to learn new skills, to do community service, or to become a stay-at-home parent (or grandparent). There is no doubt we all want greater freedom and choice in how we organize our lives, and our collective voice has the power to challenge and change the most rigid institutions (and mind-sets).

It is already clear the twenty-first century will demand more of all of us, young or old. The gifts we are given—longevity, better health, education, and financial resources—come with responsibility. After all, we have inherited and even helped create a world that needs our wisdom, experience, and compassion now. We can and must rise to the occasion. "We are not in a position in which we have nothing to work with," said psychologist Abraham Maslow,

"We already have capacities, talents, direction, missions, callings." And, as Andy Rooney opined—in a controversial *60 Minutes* essay urging older Americans to become teachers—there is, and always will be, more work than there are people to do it.

We foresee a future when stories like ours and those of other too-young-to-retire people whose stories appear here will no longer be considered unusual or remarkable. We hope for a time when everyone will be able to pursue their full potential as human beings, regardless of age. We want that for our children and theirs. Think about it. Wouldn't Mozart's music be sublime even if he weren't a "prodigy"? Can't we celebrate the genius of Grandma Moses without referring to her advanced age?

Let's work on it. Come off-road with us and let yourself be inspired by the accounts of people just like you, who have lived some and learned some, and are choosing daring adventures over the risk-adverse monotony their parents settled for.

TOP TEN WAYS TO RETIRE RETIREMENT

1. **Retire the word "retirement"** from your vocabulary. Look it up: it means to "withdraw" or "retreat." Words can shape reality, and it's time for this one to go. Doesn't "renaissance" or "graduation" or "transition" better describe your postcareer life?

2. **Realize that retirement is a relatively new concept** in human evolution. A few generations ago, before Social Security and full-time leisure became culturally embedded as the "norm," elders remained productive members of society, relied upon for their insight, wisdom, and skills.

3. **Restructure your priorities** around what is most important to you, like deepening relationships with family and friends, community service, or the arts. Now is the time to bring your professional life into line with your deeper values.

4. **Renew your zest for education.** The learning cells of your brain are hungry for new and stimulating challenges, and the welcome mat is out at many schools and universities.

5. **Revitalize your energy** by finding a community of people who embrace growth and change, and find ways to help and support each other. Don't get stuck with the "been there, done that" crowd.

6. **Rekindle your spirit for risk taking.** "Do not fear mistakes," says jazz immortal Miles Davis, "There are none." If not you, then who? If not now, when?

7. **Respond to new opportunities.** Remain open to the infinite possibilities the world has to offer. Your full potential may lie ahead.

8. **Recharge your system** by moving your body regularly. Walk, dance, swim, do yoga, take up hiking or biking. Find something you really enjoy and make it a part of your daily wellness program.

9. **Revisit your childhood dreams.** It's never too late to be who you might have been. Go for it!

10. **Remember that the wisdom** to discover and act on your deepest passion is within you.

When you are ready to get going, turn to the **Try This** sections at the end of each chapter. Think of each task listed there as a step in the right direction. Ideally, they will enable you to get to the deeper, underlying questions: What contributions have I yet to make? How might I best use the forty or more hours a week once dedicated to making a living? How am I expressing my unique talents and capabilities? Are my relationships all I want them to be? What gives my life meaning? Your true vocation, said Aristotle, lies "where your talents and the needs of the world cross." Is there any other reason to be on the planet?

You can't make a mistake, so feel free to pick and choose. Jump to any process that strikes your fancy and skip those that don't. This is *your* off-road map, and all roads lead to your personal True North. We do, however, strongly recommend that like any explorer worth his salt, you put your findings in writing. A small notebook or journal is an ideal companion for your journey. (We get our spiral-bound notebooks in an economical three-pack from the local office supply.) That way, you can refer back to it whenever you get off track or your spirits need a boost. Key point: keep moving forward.

Oh, by the way, we sold our second home in California. As an investment, it wasn't the best we've made. But for a life lesson, it was priceless.

Try This

You now know that your later life will be so different from that of your parents new words will be needed to describe it. Yet, retirement is a sacred cow not so easily disposed of. Friends and colleagues who opt for the well-trodden path to a leisure-based existence may consider you a fool for choosing otherwise. Don't be surprised by pressure to follow the herd. Whoever said cultural change would be easy? Take courage that you are not alone and seek out like-minded companions. Here are some processes we have found effective and may work for you.

- Begin with the word "retire." What do you think of when you hear or read it; what images does it conjure up for you? Write that down. Look "retire" up in the dictionary and write down the definition on one side of a new page. On the other side, write down as many antonyms as you can think of and look up the definitions. Words are powerful. Arm yourself with some that better express how you see your own future.

- What have you noticed about people who say they "can't wait to retire"? (If you don't know any, bravo!) What other characteristics do they share? What might you learn from them?

- What have you noticed about people who describe themselves as retired or semiretired? How do they spend their time and energy? Are they really idling, or just stuck with a word that has lost its meaning? What does leisure 24/7 *really* look like? Conduct some interviews and see if you can pick up common themes.

- Who comes to mind when you see the term "ageless adventurer"? Find out whatever you can about that person and write a short profile of him or her. Highlight the qualities you most admire and would like to emulate. Start creating a dream team.

- Who in your own family, now or in the past, embodies an ageless adventurer? We've been amazed at how frequently people can summon up a role model of ageless vitality. Generate a list of these personal guides and learn everything you can about each of them. Mine your own genealogy.

- In what ways do you most resemble your role model(s) for vibrant living after fifty? What questions would you most like to ask them, given the opportunity? Write down your questions and imagine the answers. Turn one into an affirmation and put it on the bathroom mirror, where you can see it every morning.

- Write yourself a new manifesto for living and attach it to the wall. Or use ours: Top Ten Ways to Retire Retirement (see sidebar).

- Write a speech to be delivered at your one hundredth birthday celebration. (Every year of zestful, engaged living improves your chances of actually delivering it personally.)

HELP WANTED

"No man is an island," said metaphysical poet John Donne. Yet independence and self-reliance are the bedrock of our national character and idealized in our popular art. We love the idea of pulling ourselves up by our own bootstraps. Even our self-help industry perpetuates the myth that we are, can, or ought to be, self-made.

Truth is, going it alone (if indeed it exists) rarely serves either individual or community. Quantum physics bears out what the ancient sacred texts have maintained all along: We are all made of the same stuff and we are interconnected in ways that may never be fully understood.

Asking for help—what author Margaret Wheatley calls "Turning to One Another"—is especially crucial for all of us already in, or anticipating, midlife and beyond. It is terra incognita. There are no precedents for a greatly expanded life span in our history, and we need each other's help in mapping it out. The sooner we learn to ask for what we need from others, the better the chance that we'll receive it. Books like this one and workshops have their place, but they are no substitute for human interaction.

Consider this, you rugged individualists: When was the last time you turned down a chance to offer assistance to someone in need? And didn't it feel great to know somebody had thought enough of you—of your skills, experience, and knowledge—to ask? They were actually paying you a huge compliment. Keep this in mind the next time you feel lost and loathe to ask for directions.

Chapter 1. Money: The Prose of Life

Money... the prose of life... hardly spoken of in parlors without an apology, is in its effects and laws, as beautiful as roses. —RALPH WALDO EMERSON

The Western dream is to have a lot of money, and then you can lead a life of leisure and happiness. Nothing in my experience could be further from the truth. —MICHAEL PHILLIPS, *The Seven Laws of Money*

Contrary to most retirement advice, making the most of the rest of your life will not depend solely on whether or not you have enough money. More important will be how well you can leverage your inherent wealth—health, creativity, experience, skills, relationships, community—into creating a life worth living. For many of us around age fifty, obsessing about money is a common theme, even for those with adequate financial resources. Why is this so? For one thing, because we live in a culture preoccupied with wealth, where many life decisions are dominated and even corrupted by the single-minded pursuit of money, it is easy to lose sight of what is really valuable. For another, it is much less risky to worry about money than to face the volcanic changes of midlife and beyond. Lastly, it takes all the self-confidence we can command to buck the prevailing—and ageist—view that we are necessarily done working, and moreover, that once we stop making money, we are worthless.

Here are two suppositions about us repeated so frequently by the mainstream financial community and virtually every personal-finance magazine that they have the weight of truth:

- We can't wait to retire. Retirement represents the "good life," a reward for a lifetime of hard labor.

- We have to amass a small fortune in order to afford retirement, and we'd better get cracking because there's no time to lose.

Let's understand that the concept of retirement itself is only a generation old. It is a by-product of the Social Security Act of 1935, designed to create jobs by moving older people out of the workforce. There is no reason to accept retirement as "conventional wisdom." It is neither. Clearly, a generation haunted by the Depression was a lot easier to convince that job security was everything, even if you hated the work, and that your reward would be "golden years" of leisure. This may be a persuasive argument when work itself is backbreaking and/or physically dangerous, but that is not the experience of the vast majority of us who made (or make) our living in the information age. Consider recent research about attitudes toward work in the fifty-plus population. An AARP survey conducted in fall 2003 found that seven of ten workers "plan to work into their retirement years or never retire . . . nearly half expect to work into their seventies or beyond." Said John Rother, director of policy and strategy for AARP, "We have never had data before that suggested people would be working that late [in life] . . . the concept of retirement is in flux." A survey done in 2000 by Rutgers University's Heldrich Center for Workforce Development found virtually the same thing. "Second Wind: Workers, Retirement, and Social Security" reported that "Workers describe a desire to continue working after full-time employment, but on their own terms. Unlike the 'work-free' retirement experienced by their parents, Americans seek a *work-filled* retirement focused on fulfilling personal goals and contributing actively to U.S. economy and society."

We believe that these findings are the result of fundamental changes in the nature of work itself today—where, when, and how work is performed—coupled with a phenomenon called "down-aging" echoed in cartoon captions and celebrity quotes: Seventy is the new fifty.

No doubt fears about money—aggravated by a roller-coaster stock market—play a role in the trend among those eligible for retirement to remain on the job longer. It may be just what the economy needs. With labor shortages looming in the coming decade, we would go so far as to say that, even if you sold your company for big bucks or got a fat inheritance from your rich uncle, it may well be your civic duty to pitch in, keep your job if you can and it suits you, or find other, more rewarding work.

E-tirement, anyone? According to Daniel Pink who coined the term in his book, *Free Agent Nation: The Future of Working for Yourself*, "Legions of sixty-plus Americans are . . . using the Internet as a platform for finding and executing work."

As it turns out, Uncle Sam wants you to extend your working life. Someone over there is paying attention to the true cost of giving up able-bodied, able-minded people to retirement. The Social Security Administration has now rolled back a complicated formula that was a disincentive to work in that it reduced benefits for every dollar earned over a certain limit. Today, the full benefits that begin at age sixty-five continue no matter how much you earn. (Of course, the earnings themselves are taxed at regular rates. Sorry.)

The Retirement Industry

The research notwithstanding, retirement is still touted as the American Dream, Act II. We're urged to "Retire Early!" "Retire Rich!" from every quarter. Howard attended one Senior Expo four years ago and is *still* getting unsolicited mail and calls from fifty-five-plus gated communities and retirement planners. To understand the consistency and persistence of the message, you have to recognize whose interests it serves. There's big money (you should pardon the expression) counting on us to pack it all in and devote the rest of our lives to leisure pursuits. The messages may be attractively packaged— youthful, if graying, couples, soaking up the sun in an exotic locale or heading off for a round of golf—but the message is the same: Get lost! Obviously, the retirement industry (traditional financial services, entertainment, leisure, travel, pharmaceuticals, and Sunbelt real estate) has much to gain in fueling the national obsession with retirement and a great deal to lose if millions of us choose otherwise. It needs to adjust its vision to one more agreeable and relevant to those whom Theodore Roszak dubbed the New People.

In the four years since we founded our Web site, 2young2retire. com, we have begun to notice signs that change is afoot. Del Webb, the developer who seeded the West with Sun Cities for the fifty-five-plus population, is now offering home designs that include a home office and high-speed Internet access. The AARP now offers career counseling through its affiliation with Drake Beam Morin, one of the nation's largest career-management organizations. These are signals that retirement as a state of permanent vacation is losing its hold on the popular imagination. That's progress.

We have no intention of retiring, a fact that needs to be taken into account in our financial calculations. Clearly, the time horizons assumed by retirement formulas don't apply to us, and need not to anyone who decides to invest *at least* as much effort into making money as to managing and preserving it. Let's put this into context. Where would you rather be? Learning new skills, interacting with other like-minded folks, and being paid for your contributions, or hunkered down with your computer, transfixed by the ups and downs of the Dow? The truth is, thousands of people of fifty, sixty, and beyond *are* heeding the advice of Stephen M. Pollan, financial and legal consultant and author of *Die Broke*, some of the smartest, most radical ideas we've come upon to reinvent our relationship with money at any age. "Don't retire," Pollan says, "Forget all the hype and marketing. Retirement isn't a golden age. It's not about doing what you want where you want. It's not a dream—it's a nightmare."

Real Security

What would happen to your prospects for living the life you want if you give your best to each day, whatever that means to you individually? We think that decision alone improves your chances to stay employed—to whatever extent you wish—but more important, keeps you *employable* in ways that mitigate inflation or a volatile stock market. That's real security, a priceless, enduring feeling of self-worth.

Listen to human potential guru Wayne Dyer: "Don't let an old person get in your skin." Millions of us within and on both sides of the Baby Boom generation are confirming that there is no shortage of opportunities to generate an income, whatever one's age, ability, and financial resources. More important are qualities like flexibility, resolve, self-confidence, and the willingness to become a beginner again if necessary.

Consider the experience of Anne Kleine of Mrs. Kleine's Krelish. A former nurse and hospice veteran, Kleine decided to open a hot-dog concession with her husband and partner, Larry. She soon saw another opportunity in the enthusiasm of customers for her "sweet" sauerkraut, a family recipe. With the help of SCORE, a volunteer organization of former executives who specialize in helping small businesses get started, Kleine scaled up production and launched her stand-alone product. It was eventually marketed throughout the Pacific Northwest, San Francisco Bay area, Ohio, and the Pittsburgh, Pennsylvania areas.

Vowing she would "never grade another paper," Ann Mariah Stewart ended thirty years as an English and history instructor at American River College in Sacramento, California, eager to launch a new career. It was a promise she wouldn't keep. Today, she splits her time between working as a park ranger at Canyonlands National Park and teaching for the navy in a program developed by Central Texas College (www.ctcd.cc.tx.us). The latest gig Stewart is considering: teaching English as a second language in China. (For more income-generating ideas, see Chapter 4: 101 Opportunities for the Open-Minded.)

"It's the Economy, Stupid!"

Money is a terrible master but an excellent servant.
> —PT BARNUM

When James Carville, the campaign strategist who helped Bill Clinton win his first election, coined the often quoted "It's the economy, stupid," he was stating something about us that we don't always like to admit. The way to our collective heart is through our wallet. We, possibly more than others in the developed world, are hung up on money and the things money can buy. For millions of Americans, writes Juliet B. Schor in *The Overspent American: Why We Want What We Don't Need*, "what they acquire and own is tightly bound to their personal identity [as] participants in a national culture of upscale spending." Of course, most retirement planning plays right into these preoccupations with material comforts and financial security.

From this, you might draw the conclusion that our money skills are as good or better than the next guy and that we understand the basic laws of money. This is far from the case. An ABCNews.com report revealed that we are surprisingly illiterate as a nation about the subject: "Americans scored an average 42 percent on a fourteen-question test of basic knowledge of personal finances. For instance, two-thirds falsely believe there is 'an organization that insures you against losing money in the stock market or as the result of investment fraud.'" (Don't we wish!) Nearly half of those tested think that diversification will protect one's investments if the stock market falls, and 63 percent don't understand the basic concept of inflation. High school seniors flubbed the math as well, with 82 percent failing basic questions on interest rates, savings, loans, credit cards, and calculating net worth. Uh-oh.

Could this be why credit card debt—$1.73 trillion now—and bankruptcies have soared to unprecedented heights in recent years? And, more to the point, why Baby Boomers, who have access to a wealth of information on personal finance, are spending money like there's no tomorrow? "I don't want to speak too disparagingly of my generation," writes Stephen King,

THE NATIONAL DEBT

Remember the National Debt Clock? The electronic billboard near Times Square intended to dramatize the federal government's red ink in numbers that scrolled by faster than the human eye could follow? Check out this symbol of government-as-compulsive-shopper. Our national debt: $6,877,326,542,456. Your share: $23,511. Ouch. (www.brillig.com/debt_clock/)

in *On Writing: A Memoir of the Craft*, "(actually I do, we had a chance to change the world and opted for the Home Shopping Network instead)."

Money Immaturity

Dysfunctional behavior around money in the form of uncontrollable spending and runaway debt may be this generation's cross to bear. But money madness has other forms, on both ends of the wealth scale. Raised in Appalachia, George D. Kinder, a fee-only certified financial planner and author of *Seven Stages of Money Maturity: Understanding the Spirit and Value of Money in Your Life*, saw his hardworking attorney father struggle to make money. So devastating was the memory that when Kinder graduated from Harvard in 1971 with a degree in English literature, he was determined he wasn't going to sacrifice his soul "in any pursuit as unfulfilling as a 'job.'" Instead, he would spend "the better part of the next decade resisting and rejecting the idea of a career, setting aside my natural aptitudes in financial affairs for a vain attempt to become an artist."

"When I married, my wife and I made a deal. First, she would support me for two years, while I pursued my writing and artwork, and studied the soul. Then I would return the favor." When the two years were up, his wife "claimed her half of the bargain. Again I faced the demand of earning money. The old suffering came back," he said. Like the clients Kinder works with today, he found himself holding on "to a body of beliefs with such fierceness and misplaced loyalty that they block us from the experience and pursuit of freedom, often for years, sometimes for our whole life."

Wait a minute. Isn't freedom what money is supposed to bring us—what our "dues-paying" is about?

Kinder's insights about money and suffering ring true in our own lives, and may in yours. At nineteen, Howard got a message about financial success at any price that shaped his own youthful rebellion against gainful employment and created long-standing misgivings about money. His father, a typical first-generation American for whom life was about "making it" in business, collapsed and died of a heart attack at age forty-nine. He had enjoyed early success and made a lot of money, moving the family to an affluent neighborhood filled with other entrepreneurs. Then came two business failures, the stress of a six-day workweek to keep up with the bills, and loss of self-esteem that he never regained. After his death, the family moved into more modest accommodations, and Howard's mother, at age fifty, took a service job. Howard eventually found his vocation in advertising sales, but until recently, studiously avoided becoming an entrepreneur.

Marika's father—a career diplomat, enjoying a state-provided house, servants, and chauffeur-driven car—suddenly found himself on the wrong side of his employer, stripped of citizenship, job, and home, and "down to his last $1,000." Although within a year, he had begun a new career as a college professor, he was haunted by his earlier losses and preoccupied with rebuilding financial security. Her parents always lived far more frugally than was necessary, renting rather than buying a home, although they had both opportunity and means, driving the same modest car until it fell apart, traveling infrequently, and making other sacrifices to create a financial safety net. The abrupt change in her parents' fortune left Marika with heavy-duty issues around money and security that she is still working through.

Denial, fear, overwork, low self-esteem, penny-pinching, stress, suffering. No one would deliberately choose any of these, yet they are often strange bedfellows in our relationship with money. To what degree are unconscious scripts about money and security from earlier in your life, or from another era altogether, driving the

WORLDS WITHOUT MONEY

We are all familiar with baby-sitting clubs and carpools as examples of nonmonetary exchanges that benefit all concerned. We have an airport car-service exchange in our condo community. About once a month or so, someone gets a free ride to or pick up from the airport, courtesy of a friendly neighbor, with good conversation as a premium. The idea of using "social capital" instead of money is formalized in a concept called "Time Dollars," invented by Washington, D.C., attorney Edgar Cahn in 1986 at the London School of Economics. "Market economics values what is scarce, not the real work of society, which is caring, loving, being a citizen, a neighbor and a human being. That work will, I hope, never be so scarce that the market value goes high, so we have to find a way of rewarding contributions to it." Check out the Time Dollar Institute Web site: www.timedollar.org. Inspiring.

decisions you're making in maturity? Are you, as poet e.e. cummings quipped, "living so far beyond my income that we may almost be said to be living apart." Spendthrift or tightwad, we use money as a stand-in for what's missing in our lives: needs we haven't satisfied; goals we haven't met; the whole category of unfinished business that becomes more urgent around age fifty.

Despite what bestsellers like Robert Kiyosaki's *Rich Dads Retire Young, Retire Rich* suggest, merely having more money won't permanently change or improve any of those things. Rich or poor, goes an old saying, you still have to put your pants on, one leg at a time. Reflect on the First Law of Money from Michael Phillips's *The Seven Laws of Money*: "The values in your life have to be powerful, tangible values that exist independently of money." The other six laws according to Phillips, developer of Master-Card and a former high-ranking banking executive, are also worth your consideration.

When we invest in understanding and clearing up the emotional baggage money brings to the surface—no overnight task for most of us—it's just possible the money will take care of itself. It's no miracle. Just remind yourself that money is a medium of exchange with no intrinsic value. If we didn't have money, we would have to invent it, like convicts using cigarettes for currency. Money, the "prose of life," exists to serve us, not dominate our existence.

A Financial Adviser of Your Own

It used to be that when you made your first appointment with a financial adviser or retirement counselor, you would be asked to bring in a balance sheet and other detailed statements of your net worth. That's still true and necessary, but thanks to innovators like George Kinder and Richard B. Wagner, former chair of the Institute of Certified Financial Planners (now Financial Planning Association), those conversations are becoming more comprehensive and holistic—a little like confession, without the need for absolution.

In 1994, Kinder and Wagner cofounded the Nazrudin Project named for the Mullah Nazrudin, a character in Sufi stories who comes up with unconventional solutions to problems. An informal fraternity of influential certified financial planners (CFPs), including past presidents of the ICFP, that meets each year, the group addresses the "soul of money" and the best ways to help clients understand the connection between money, sex, and power, and how it can damage relationships and get in the way of sound, financial management. "Money skills are the survival skills of the twenty-first century," Wagner believes. In turbulent times like these, we need to brush up on the New Math.

Today, anyone with a computer and a dial-up Internet connection can tinker with their portfolio online, so financial planners know they have to offer clients more to build the solid, long-term relationships they need to thrive in business. There is a distinct advantage to having someone like Kinder, Wagner, or Stephen Pollan on your team, so shop around until you're satisfied you have found an enlightened professional. Both the Institute of Certified Financial Planners (icfp@icfp.org) and the National Association of Personal Financial Advisers can help you find a fee-only planner in your area. As you probably guessed, "fee-only" means the financial planner doesn't get his or her compensation on commission and is therefore able to give you an objective opinion as opposed to promoting a specific product. Check with friends. Call around until you find a CFP who talks your language. Set up a meeting and ask him or her to run the numbers for you on several scenarios, including what your finances might look like if you continue to contribute to Social Security and postpone taking your benefits until the compulsory age of seventy. In addition to the financial statement, prepare for your meeting by working up as detailed a plan for your life as you can manage. Attend the meeting with your mate or life partner and also include him or her in the preliminary discussions. Don't let those columns and rows get you down; it's only money. Include this document in your preparations and you'll be well on your way to getting treated as an individual, not a member of an age group. Expect the best and increase your chances of receiving it.

DO WELL/DO GOOD

Corporate scandals heighten the need for due diligence when it comes to investing. After all, as stockholders (via individual stocks or mutual funds), we own a piece of a company, for better or worse, but not necessarily forever. If you prefer not to do your own research, here's a way to ensure your investments align with your values. It's called "socially responsible investing" (SRI), a method of screening investment vehicles so you invest only in companies whose products and services contribute to a just, sustainable society, and avoid those who don't. Here are some of the "screens" for responsible investing created by Co-op America (www.coopamerica.org):

- Environmental record: policies and programs

- Labor and employment: Equal Opportunity, employee relations, fair labor bargaining

- Race and Gender Equity

- Safe, durable products; support for education and community.

You can also learn how to become an activist shareholder to promote responsible corporate behavior. Hold $1,000 worth of a company's stock for a year and you can sponsor resolutions at the annual shareholders meeting.

SRI needn't hurt your portfolio, either. Check the Mutual Fund Performance Chart at www.socialinvest.org/areas/sriguide/mfpc.cfm. According to the Social Investment Forum News, "Of the 18 socially screened funds with more than $100 million in assets, 13 received top rankings from either Lipper and Morningstar or both" through the first half of 2002.

Had Enough?

For many of us, realizing that we can make an income is one way to tackle our scarcity fears. But there is another breathtakingly simple yet powerful strategy that has worked for thousands of people: coming to terms with what, for you, is enough. Try saying the word "enough" aloud. What comes into your mind? What happens in your body? All successful diets work by retraining our bodies to feel satisfied with a lower calorie intake. We can apply the same principle of "enoughness" to our financial life.

Here is a little secret from the Voluntary Simplicity movement the retirement industry would just as soon you don't find out: You can live far more comfortably with less than you thought possible, and, even more radical, *you are free to choose*. As long as you pay your taxes and curb your dog, what you decide to spend your money on is up to you. If you find yourself worrying about keeping up appearances, bear in mind this simple advice from Fred Rogers of *Mister Rogers' Neighborhood*: Don't be concerned about what others think of you. You'd be surprised how little they do.

Consider this an invitation to experiment with the other side of the equation: not income (chances are you have a good handle on that), but where your money goes. First, stash the plastic, yes, the ATMs too, and start paying cash like your parents used to do. Keep one card in a safe place for emergencies, like unexpected home repairs or urgent travel, and always pay it off before it comes due. It's like a free 25- or 30-day loan. "Credit cards are one of the primary battlegrounds on which you have to fight for your economic life," advises die-broke advocate, Stephen Pollan, "Remove every credit card from your wallet, including gasoline cards. There's absolutely no reason you need to carry them around. The only things they do is make it easier for you to ignore prices and buy things you don't need and can't afford." Tough medicine with no sugar coating. We took Pollan's advice and have been amazed at how quickly using cash or a check (one, tucked into a wallet for emergencies) has made us more aware of our spending habits and helped us control them. Bottom line, it works.

When you pay cash and keep the receipts, you have an immediate record of your expenses. To avoid replacing one obsessive behavior over money with another, try making a game out of keeping track of your money. A little lightness around this subject never hurt.

Simply Rich

Enough-ness wasn't the goal of fifty-somethings Jim and Kendra Golden, an engineer and lawyer, respectively, who quit their jobs, sold their home of twenty years, and headed West in a thirty-two-foot RV to look for America and a new, less stressful, more meaningful life. However, it was one of the off-road discoveries that changed the way they think about money and how they spend it.

As Kendra Golden tells it, life "on board" was simple. They concentrated on seeing and doing all the things they could find of interest in the places visited that were free or inexpensive—outdoor activities, local museums, art galleries, music and theater offered by local colleges, self-guided walking tours, and window-shopping. The couple found that traveling in a motor home made it easy not to buy things because space was limited. They also enjoyed cooking for themselves rather than taking a chance on whatever restaurant they came across. They camped or parked overnight at free or inexpensive sites. They reported themselves "interested (and pleased) to see how significantly we have reduced our living expenses," and how richly they were living in experiences, new friends, and opportunities. Eventually the Goldens found a little town in the Pacific Northwest that met their criteria for the good life and settled there.

Children's book author Rita Golden Gelman has taken an even

more radical approach to her financial life. Divorced, with two grown sons, Gelman decided to blend her passion for travel and exploring other cultures with the desire to live more frugally. In her book, *Tales of a Female Nomad: Living at Large in the World*, she describes how she manages to live on about $10,000 a year by making her home in places like Bali, where the average civil servant makes $50 a month (the equivalent of our monthly cell-phone service!), which puts things in perspective.

The odysseys of Gelman and the Goldens are not for everyone, but they do teach us what is possible when we base life decisions on something other than money. Like these adventurers, we can understand where our money is going and what it is buying us— one of the most liberating things we can do at any age. Frankly, it takes resolve and daily reinforcement to rid ourselves of nonstop consuming so attractively packaged as The American Way of Life. Our economy depends heavily on the Consumer Confidence Index. Scary, when you realize that the so-called confidence of consumers is closely tied to the stratospheric rise of credit card debt.

Putting Money in Its Place

Accept that money is part of life, neither the most important part nor something we can avoid. Face the fact that we all have emotional issues around money and the time to do something about them is right now. Talk them out with your life partner, if you have one, sign up for a seminar or hire a personal coach skilled in such matters. It's what you don't know that can hurt you. Tackle the practical details of your finances without delay. Create a simple record-keeping system that encourages you to document every amount above a figure you find significant. That's anything over $5 for us. Start paying attention to your spending and make sure you're getting your money's worth in the best sense of the term. *Your Money or Your Life: Transform-*

ing Your Relationship with Money and Achieving Financial Independence, the groundbreaking book by Vicki Robin and the late Joe Dominguez, has some excellent exercises to help measure what something costs you in life energy. Find out if you are making a living or, as Dominguez and Robin mordantly suggest, "making a dying." Small, resolute steps like these not only make practical sense, but can add up to financial independence and freedom later in life. That's wealth an accountant might have difficulty accounting for.

And there are other, equally important advantages as Rita Gelman and Jim and Kendra Golden discovered. You may learn what contributes to your sense of abundance or enoughness, a psychological and spiritual bonus if there ever was one. You may learn to distinguish between what you need to live well and what is window dressing. As for the excess, the stuff you couldn't do without—for many of us, literally the accumulation of twenty or thirty years—there's eBay, the popular online auction site. Arguably, eBay performs a valuable recycling service, but would it exist at all if we stopped buying stuff we don't need? Log on and get an eyeful of where America's impulse buying-on-credit ends. Just don't succumb to auction fever, okay?

Adopt an entrepreneur's perspective toward the rest of your life. You're going to have a lot to work with, after all. That might encourage you to create a financial reserve equal to 6–12 months of your expenses (the advice of virtually every financial planner) and to bring your expenses in line with your income (the "secret" to prosperity, say the ancient sages). You won't know until you try. Get out that yellow, lined pad and sharpen your pencil.

A LESSON FROM MONOPOLY

Remember playing Monopoly as a kid? The only thing you could count on was that $200 you collected when you passed Go. The rest—fortune or failure—depended on the roll of the dice. We're not in any way advocating gambling here; in fact, we believe that gambling, whether in state lotteries or upscale casinos, is the biggest fool's game ever perpetrated on the population. But Monopoly is a game that has a lot to teach us about money and life.

1. Money itself has no value. It is a utility, like electricity or water. How we use it determines its value to us. Money is a medium of exchange: We use it to acquire goods or services for whatever someone has determined they are worth.
2. Money you don't spend accumulates.
3. When you have money in reserve, you can act on opportunities that come your way.
4. Never overextend yourself.
5. Don't play with money that isn't yours.
6. Win or lose, it's the people you play with that make the game interesting.
7. Have fun or find another game.

Try This

- An exorcism ritual. Think about a time when you had a serious disappointment about money. Maybe the raise or windfall you were expecting didn't come about, or someone cheated or robbed you. What is happening in your body as you bring that thought to mind? The feelings are real even if the circumstances were in the past. Get those issues out of your tissues! Write them down on a separate piece of paper, then shred, burn, or deep-six it.

- Finish this sentence: "If I had all the money I needed, I would . . ." Start a new section in your notebook called "Money," and make a list of everything that comes to mind. Keep going until you run out of steam. Then choose one and examine it more carefully.

  How important is the money, really?

  Where and how in your life are you already expressing this heart's desire? (Hint: look beyond the obvious.)

  Write your answers in your notebook or journal. Consider making a poster of any important insights and fastening it to your refrigerator, next to your grocery list and the photos of your grandchildren, best buddies, or beloved pets.

- Here's a technique borrowed from the classic, *Your Money or Your Life*. For the next four weeks, keep a daily record of everything you spend. Carry around a pocket tape recorder or your trusty notebook and pen. Make a game of catching it all, from the small change you used for the morning paper, to that cup of latte you couldn't resist, to the bigger items, like the rent or mortgage payment. You may find yourself wanting to cheat after the novelty wears off. Don't.

- As an experiment, for the next four weeks (at least), quarantine the plastic and pay cash for all your purchases (excluding the basics like rent or mortgage, utilities, etc., which you pay by check). Even better, draw an amount of cash to cover your weekly expenses and make do. Be disciplined. Jot down any positive changes you notice in your spending patterns, and reward yourself in a way that doesn't involve spending money, e.g., a walk in the park, gallery browsing, making music or art (yes, you can!), writing a letter to an old friend.

- Beginning on a new page, draw a vertical line down the middle to create two columns. Title one column "Needs" and the other "Wants." Divide your expense record into the two columns. Pretty revealing, huh?

  Now pick one item from your "Wants" column and make a list or write a short paragraph about the last time you bought something you didn't really need, how it made you feel, and for how long. Sometimes retail therapy can lift the spirit. Just understand what the motivation is.

- Go through your home and inventory all the things you own that you neither like nor use. This is your money turned into stuff. In your notebook (which is filling up nicely by now), create three categories: 1. use and enjoy now, e.g., the "good silver" or special-occasion linens; 2. donate to charity (remember to get a receipt for your taxes); 3. dump. Set a deadline for acting on all three or, if that sounds impossible, hire a professional organizer to help you. Find one via the National Association of Professional Organizers at www.napo.net.

- For more great ideas, check www.ihatefinancialplanning.com for their exercise on finding your "Money Personality."

Chapter 2.
It's Not Working

Find a job you like and you add five days to every week.
—H. JACKSON BROWN, JR.

One of the symptoms of an approaching nervous breakdown is the belief that one's work is terribly important.
—BERTRAND RUSSELL

As long as we're retiring retirement, let's work on work. After all, we now know that work—full-time, part-time, flextime, on our own time—is likely to be a part of our lives for many more years because 1. we *can*, and even *want* to work, thanks to better health and prospects for a longer life, and 2. we are needed. Although more experienced (and expensive) workers take the hit in economic downturns, we are one answer to labor shortages expected to arrive within the decade, according to the U.S. Department of Labor. This is why a respected organization like The Conference Board was studying issues of retention of "preretirees"—people 45–55—in 2001 and talking about creating an "ageless workforce." And why the AARP, long associated with looking out for the rights of retired people, recently launched a high-profile campaign to identify and recognize companies most hospitable to its fifty-plus membership.

Will the "graying of the workforce" change the workplace? Inevitably, and for the better, in much the same way that racial and cultural diversity enriches and strengthens society as a whole. Ageism, whether subtle or overt, hurts both those who suffer discrimination and those who practice it. The ship of state needs all hands on deck.

The nature of work itself is evolving and becoming more difficult to classify or measure. We might agree that work still means payment for services rendered, but the where, when, and how are up for grabs. What is the "thinking time" we devote to an exciting project if not work? What about a brainstorming lunch with a colleague or an impromptu meeting on one's own time? Or is it only called work if we'd rather be doing something—anything—else? Can work be play? Fun? Rewarding for its own sake? The technological revolution is credited with accelerating work and eliminating jobs. But computers and telecommunications have also spawned a diversity of work styles, innovation, and creativity unimaginable a generation ago. Consider how quaintly inadequate labels like "blue collar" or "white collar" are in describing the way many jobs are performed in the information age. We are all using more brain than brawn these days to do the job efficiently. Women and minorities are breaking the glass ceiling, and real men not only eat quiche, they are as likely to prepare it at home or at the helm of a four-star

SO, WHAT DO YOU DO?

In Henry Higgins's world, an Englishman's way of speaking absolutely classified him. In ours, we draw a similar conclusion from what a person does for a living. "So, what do you do?" we are quick to ask—rushing in where many other cultures fear to tread. Once upon a time in the industrial dark ages, the type of work you did determined where you lived, shopped, who your friends were, even the brand of beer you drank and whether you were on a bowling league or joined the golf club. Today, in our more fluid society, all bets are off. We are not our jobs.

restaurant. So work will continue to mutate for the foreseeable future, and that is, or should be, music to our ears.

Time-Out

One thing that is due for a drastic overhaul is the outsize value we assign to work (and, on the flip side, to playing hard and/or retiring early). One measure of workaholism in North America is the number of hours we spend on the job, whether we are physically on site or not. A few years ago, a study by the Families and Work Institute showed that the average American male works forty-nine hours a week (women work forty-two). In fact, we know fifty, sixty, and more hours a week are so common, particularly in the service industries that now dominate our economy, that they have been accepted as normal. Of course, this doesn't include commuting and the stuffed briefcase you tote home evenings and weekends. How "hard" one works still carries a certain cachet in our culture, but here's how it adds up in real time: We spend an additional three months on the job each year, or two weeks longer than the Japanese and two months more than the Germans.

If we're spending most of our waking hours at a job that nurtures and rewards our unique talents and abilities, that may not seem a bad bargain. But love our work or hate it, those extra hours have to add up, stealing time and energy from our intimate relationships, communities, and other important parts of life. What are we working for? To what do our efforts contribute? Are we using our talents and skills to full advantage? In what ways does our work line up with our deepest values? Are we having fun? Who has time to ask?

Clearly, it's not working for millions of the overworked. Any unhealthy relationship is not sustainable. Something has to give and does, in burnout or some variation of it. Features about finding

AMERICA THE OVERWORKED

Average Annual Vacation Days:

United States	13
Japan	25
Canada	26
Great Britain	28
Brazil	34
Germany	35
France	37
Italy	42

balance have multiplied in popular magazines and on *Oprah*; and coach Cheryl Richardson's *Take Time for Your Life* is a bestseller. "Despite everything our inheritance may tell us, work is not and never has been the center of the human universe," says poet and author David Whyte (*The Heart Aroused: Poetry and the Preservation of Soul in Corporate America*), "and the universe, with marvelous compassion, seems willing to take endless pains to remind us of that fact."

An Off-Road Look at Downsizing

The good news is, you still have a job. The bad news is, you still have a job. Regardless of which side your cubicle or corner office happens to be when the ax falls, it's never pretty. Downsizing has disrupted thousands of lives and sown bitterness and distrust of Corporate America, much of it richly deserved as recent scandals show. Proponents (usually those with jobs and power) justify layoffs as necessary medicine, a strategy for maintaining a competitive position in the global economy. Critics call it folly. Virtually all agree we ain't seen nothing yet.

Downsizing isn't going away for the simple reason that it produces results for those who measure success or failure in the corporate bottom line or quarterly shareholders' report (you shareholders take note). That's the same culture that gave birth to the Organization Man and his progeny: workers ready to sacrifice personal freedom and integrity for so-called job security and guaranteed lifetime employment. We know what extraordinary courage it takes to rock the boat (let alone blow the whistle). And what complicates being laid off for us Americans is that, unlike Canadians and Europeans with some form of national health insurance, we and our families become exposed to financial risk our luckier neighbors never have to face—a good reason to fight for reform of our health-care system if there ever was one.

If you are among the newly downsized, skip the denial phase and give these remedies a shot:

1. Grieve, cry, break a sweat, give that punching bag at the gym a workout. Get the rage (feeling of betrayal, fear, etc.) out of your system physically before it gets you.
2. Call a family conference. Assure everyone that you will all survive, but be up front with them that sacrifices may be necessary in the short term. Enlist the help of everyone.
3. Swallow your pride and apply for unemployment. Make sure your health benefits continue under COBRA while you research other possibilities.
4. Create a new mission statement. It's a big mistake to assume your next job will necessarily come from the industry you know or the contacts you already have.
5. When you feel ready to plunge back in, put as much time into your new quest as you did in your previous job. But this time, make it fun.

For more good ideas, some frivolous, many worth the price of admission, check out Monster.com's "100 Things to Do If You've Been Laid Off." (http://content.monster.com/careerchangers/articles/advice_for_the_jobless/100things/)

Before you begin papering the walls of recruiters in your former industry with your resumes, consider a model that works for our

---

THE 2YOUNG2RETIRE CREDO

1. As human beings, we have the right to work that is safe, decent, and adequately compensated.
2. However, no job is an entitlement. (The same goes for retirement.)
3. Even if you love your work (and we're in favor of that), a job is just a job, a way of making the money you need to live. Not life itself, and certainly not *you*. How to pursue happiness? Let us count the ways.

---

children and younger colleagues. Like it or not, serial careers, multiple employers, project and contract work are the order of the day. The fact is, these strategies foster independence, resilience, and a sense of your own value, not so easily dislodged by external events. Give up the myth of the secure job and open yourself to something more irreplaceable: self-worth. If you can't become an entrepreneur, behave like one.

We believe comic Jackie Mason was on to something when he opined that America would be in far better shape if members of Congress were put on commission. If we become more like the freelancers of old, perhaps we (and employers in the long run) will be the better for it. Daniel Pink (*Free Agent Nation*) believes that work and the workplace are already being shaped by a growing number of free agents whose loyalty is no longer to a single company, but to themselves and an ad hoc cadre of peers coming together for a mutually beneficial project, then dispersing and regrouping as needed, what Pink calls "the Hollywood model."

A Declaration of Independence

Artists have always had a leg up on independent action and have much to teach us. Our friend, British writer and television producer Guy Slater, has built a successful career running a regional theater, developing and producing series for the BBC (his *Love Hurts* with

Zoe Wannamaker was a huge hit and his earlier *Miss Marple* series is still in circulation), writing children's books, novels, and radio plays, and more recently, a screenplay for a full-length film. Once, when money was particularly tight, he turned actor in a small role in *I, Claudius*, the legendary *Masterpiece Theater* series. He also managed to raise a family, buy a house, pay his taxes, serve on the prestigious Arts Council of England, and in his fifties, take a six-month sabbatical to replenish his creative juices.

Sound impossible? Not so for you free agents in the making. Here's a story from Marika's recent past. As a freelance writer, she had an eleven-year relationship with an old-school Fortune 500 company. Its employees enjoyed opportunities for training and the best benefits package in the industry. Promotions came from within, so employees tended to be "lifers." When the first layoffs were announced—albeit a kinder, gentler version—people were incredulous at first, then those with the right numbers—age and seniority—led an exodus. Everyone survived, but those who had more irons in the fire to begin with, as moonlighting teachers, aspiring playwrights or, in one case, working a small farm, were better off a year or two later than those who had allowed themselves to become dependent on the mother ship.

Marika's personal life raft in the eventual loss of this large client was made up of the skills acquired while on contract (computer competence, for one thing), a reputation for doing good work that helped her compete for that next "gig," and a network of people she could approach to keep the pump primed for future assignments. Luckily, her toolbox contained a version of what Tom Peters calls "Three Rs for the '90s": Reputation, Resume, and Rolodex (in his recent *The Pursuit of Wow! Every Person's Guide to Topsy-Turvy Times*).

The irony is, just as Corporate America is shooting itself in its collective foot by laying off its most experienced workers, it is also hurting for people with imagination, creativity, flexibility, and resilience. With some attitude adjustment you, the fifty-something, skilled, mature, laid-off worker of today could be reborn as tomorrow's crackerjack project director, consultant, or supplier of just-in-time goods or services, if you so choose.

The New Entrepreneurs

The True Stories profiles collected in the 2young2retire Web site (most of them submitted unsolicited) have given us a window on the workstyles of the fifty-plus, and confirm what we have lived through ourselves. Most of the eighty or so people we profiled have blazed their own trails as entrepreneurs (and creators of jobs for others) and independent contractors. We know that it is not always a smooth ride and not every venture is blessed with financial success. Yet we believe that our experience and that of many others like us confirms a trend identified by Tom Peters, Daniel Pink, and other observers of the workplace: work as we have known it for most of the twentieth century is gasping its last, which means that retirement in the sense it has been understood since 1935, is most certainly defunct. Good riddance to both. Welcome to the new entrepreneurs.

For Paul Zapka, a former human-resources executive with Lipton Tea (a household name that still calls up cozy images), downsizing—as "psychologically debilitating" as it was—proved the opportunity to be reborn as the principal in the Human Resource Advantage Inc., "a general-management consulting firm focused on organization effectiveness: Linking Capability and Growth." Walking away from his employer before age fifty-five cost Zapka an estimated $700,000 in pension, health care, and other benefits. Yet, "I am definitely better off as an entrepreneur than if I would have remained in traditional employment, primarily from a psychological/

emotional perspective. My last three years in the corporate environment were absolutely the worst years of my business life," he says.

"The two things most important to starting my own business were my network and the ability to create a value proposition for services I market. The importance of a well-developed network cannot be overstated. My network serves as a resource from two perspectives: 1. It has served as kind of an informal board of directors, providing independent, objective input/advice to business decision making, a sounding board, and direction on what sets me apart from others, my Unique Selling Point (USP); 2. It has provided a base to build the business, providing me with both opportunities to provide a service (i.e., work) and with referrals to potential clients."

After 9/11, Human Resource Advantage "went ten months without any new revenue," but business is improving. "When things are going good, you have to be fiscally responsible to survive unforeseen downturns in the economy. I'm happy to say that although it was getting close, no one will have to throw a benefit for my wife and me yet!

"Nothing compares to the exhilaration of starting something on your own and knowing that success lies in your own hands, not someone else's. Since I started a consulting business and the principal product is me (i.e., my intellectual capital), success has provided a much-needed ego boost. Starting a business has been both an intellectual and emotional challenge, but richly rewarding."

PROMOTE YOURSELF

If you have traded in your monthly commuter pass for a home office, you are one of many who are striking out on their own, perhaps for the first time. Whether you are a consultant, a freelance writer, or graphics designer, or whether you've turned your skill with a skillet into a new catering enterprise, chances are you are largely dependent on yourself to bring in the business. You will need to spread the word to prospective clients, letting them know who you are, what you have to offer, and why you deserve their serious consideration.

Unless billboards or an advertising campaign fit your style and budget, public relations may be your best option. So how do you go about it? Ilise Benun, author of *Self-Promotion Online: Marketing Your Creative Services Using Web Sites, E-mail and Digital Portfolios* (North Light Books, 2001) has some ideas for you. A national speaker and consultant on new-business development for small businesses, she also teaches courses online at www.selfpromotiononline.com. Her article in 2young2retire.com, www.2young2retire.com/ilisecol1.htm, is a primer on public relations for the beginner—and who isn't a beginner in this brave, new world of instant communications and information overload?

In 1978, when Henry and Isabel Coryat, owners and chief artisans of Coryat Casting Company Inc., established their bronze-sculpture foundry in Rhinebeck, New York, they never dreamed it would become the flourishing venture it is today. Henry was at the peak of a twenty-three-year career in international banking and finance, and Isabel owned an art gallery/frame shop. They prepared for their new business with a one-year apprenticeship at the Johnson Atelier Technical Institute of Sculpture in Mercerville, New Jersey. Then the Coryats bought a residential/commercial building in Rhinebeck, New York; built and outfitted their art foundry entirely by themselves within the commercial part of the building (all 3,750 square feet of it)—at which time they completely ran out of money. Ready or not, they declared themselves open for business.

Says Henry: "It may be hard for some to understand why or how two people, who had grown accustomed to living luxuriously (large villa, servant, cook, Mercedes, large salary, first-class air travel, long vacations, etc.) would decide to give up those creature comforts and financial security for a life of hard work; risk of failure with consequent loss of time and investment; and an income which could at best provide them by comparison with a relatively modest lifestyle. This can be explained only by our shared love of art, a passion to make beautiful, tangible things with our own hands, and a desire to work together at an activity we both find completely fulfilling. In our fondest dreams, we never envisioned that not only would we achieve success as an art foundry, but that we would also be selected as the foundry exclusively entrusted by The Metropolitan Museum of Art to produce their bronze reproductions."

The Coryats were driven to change their work and lives by their passion for art. For Paul Zapka and a sixty-seven-year-old, involuntarily retired woman named Betty Fox, of Bayside, New York, necessity proved to be the mother of invention. Laid off for the second time, she wasn't looking for a new career or business, she just wanted to keep herself engaged. So with an MSNTV setup provided by her computer-whiz son Marty, she made her first foray into cyberspace, searching for a recipe for peach pie. She typed "peaches" into a search engine and pulled up 85,870 pages—everything from online porn to peach wholesalers. So the widow and grandmother decided single-handedly to tame the chaos of the Internet for people of her age. Her Web site www.grandmabetty.com went online in September 1998 with some original material and hundreds of links to other sites precisely categorized: entertainment, government, health, investing, travel, magazines, memorabilia, news, and weather, to name a few. Hundreds of people visit her free site everyday, and she has become a much sought-after speaker. Her self-published book *When One Door Closes...Another Opens* is her latest endeavor.

What can we learn from the experiences of Paul Zapka, Henry and Isabel Coryat, Betty Fox, and scores of other mature workers who are making their way in a world unknown to their parents' generation? For one thing, these examples of people's innate resilience and spunk deserve equal weight in the almost uniformly tragic reporting on downsizing (see "The Downsizing of America," *The New York Times*, 1996). We believe there is, or could be, more to life than jobs "as secure as civil service posts," a good life dependent on higher salaries, "new cars, nice vacations, and unbridled trips to the mall," and what Michael Phillips (*The Seven Laws of Money*) calls "lusting for retirement." Rock on.

Love's Labor Found

At fifty, we get a birthday greeting few of us welcome without qualification: a personalized invitation to join the AARP. How the heck do they know? Maybe we take it in stride—although going ballistic is not out of the question either. The passage of time is no news to us, after all. Haven't we been paying more attention to ads for skincare products and cosmetic surgery and, if we've been of the couch-potato persuasion, exercise? From a recent advertorial in *The New York Times*: "Baby Boomers have discovered Botox, the 'fountain of youth in a syringe.'"

What is of more practical value, however, is the change *inside* our heads: potential employers and/or business partners take note. Unless forced by financial necessity, few of us will settle for just another job in our mature years. "Most workers see their 'retirement' not as a time for leisure and travel, but as an opportunity to do fulfilling work, and find avocation in what they do," says the Rutgers University's Heldrich Center for Workforce Development study. Truth is, if many of us are hungry for work that is meaningful and satisfying on many levels, we are simply responding to an instinct that may be hardwired into our maturing psyches. Many traditions, Native American and Buddhist among them, recognize that midlife is the time to take on "life's work."

We spend the first half of our lives learning what we love—we should find a way to do those things the second half.
—DAVID WHYTE

Two weeks shy of his fiftieth birthday in 1988, Bob Griffiths, author of *Do What You Love for the Rest of Your Life: A Practical Guide to Career Change and Personal Renewal* (Ballantine Books, 2001) left his position as a senior vice president of LF Rothschild and Company, the height of a long career in the financial markets. Despite a quick climb up the ladder at household names like Citibank and Merrill Lynch, he had concluded: "I wasn't cut out for the business world. It was not a natural fit." He was drawn to the theater ("my first love"), to playwriting, then acting and directing. He also considered the possibility of a helping profession such as counseling.

But before he could do anything, he had to get out of what he calls "The Consumption Trap" in his book. "I had made a lot of money and spent even more, so that after I made my decision to leave Wall Street, it took me five years to pay off all my debts and put some money aside." Since then, Griffiths's professional life in and out of the theater has blossomed. One of his plays got its first Actors Equity production in 1992, a West Coast premiere in 1995 that garnered "great reviews" from the *Los Angeles Times*, and an

Off-Broadway premiere in 1998. He was commissioned to write three original plays in 1996 (which he also directed), and has gone on to win three national playwriting awards.

Today, he is author, actor, musician, professional speaker, and teacher. He has also discovered "a wonderful spiritual life, which began during an emotional and spiritual crisis nineteen years ago," as he witnessed friends and Wall Street colleagues become devastated by downsizing, burnout, frustration, and deteriorating health. "Fulfillment and happiness are a by-product of how I live my life; they don't arrive (for me) by spending all day on a golf course. I'm not supposed to 'retire' and vegetate!"

A BUSINESS BUILT FOR TWO

Like many newish entrepreneurs, we work out of a home-based office. As you might suspect, it's not always a pretty picture, but we manage well enough for the moment. We have separate workspaces—mandatory, unless you have a very large room you can dedicate to the business. Most of the time, we observe a church/state separation of responsibilities. Marika does all the writing for 2young2retire; Howard does development work, which means everything else. Whenever one of us gets impatient with our progress, we remind ourselves that Steve Jobs launched the personal computer revolution in a garage.

To work live *and* work together, you have to be able to lighten up and laugh frequently. Here are a few more golden rules:

1. Never discuss business in the bedroom. Ours already doubles (triples?) as the reading corner, the TV room, even the crumbly snack—and-TV room. Set down a boundary on talking shop here. (Trust us on this one.)

2. Have a business plan, but prepare to make changes in it as your enterprise grows and evolves. If nothing else, a plan helps clarify your vision and keeps you on track. Without one, you run the risk of reacting to whatever comes along; you have a more difficult time distinguishing between what furthers the goal and what distracts from it. Small businesses, like big ones, need to get the forest/trees perspective right.

3. Let the talents/interests/tendencies of each partner determine who does what. Howard is the idea guy, the visionary, the resident optimist, with a classic lemonade-from-lemons outlook. Gregarious, outgoing, he's the perfect front man. Marika prefers the role of behind-the-scenes strategist. She likes learning new things, solving problems, and helping people. She needs lots of quiet to balance her life.

4. Impose a structure on your work. Even though we're around each other 24/7, we schedule meetings for specific purposes,

yellow, lined pads, decaf, the whole bit. A structure helps to avoid duplicating effort and minimizes the chance of important tasks falling through the cracks. We decide who is going to follow up on what and put it on the calendar. We can see building a larger team on these principles.

5. Take time out when you don't discuss business at all. When the business itself is fun and/or fast-paced, you have to work at creating no-work zones. But it's worth it. We remind ourselves that there's a lot more at stake here than whether our business succeeds or fails. We also try to take breaks during the day to walk, stretch (a short yoga series is great), have a snack, do the crossword.

5. Agree to consult on and make all the big decisions together. Let the smaller decisions be made by the one chiefly responsible, then stand by that decision. Of course, this is rarely so cut and dried, but it helps to have the intention.

6. Above all, be flexible, have fun, laugh. If you're like us, you've done work in the past that you haven't always enjoyed. Now is the time to have the time of your life, in work that is meaningful and closer to your heart.

How might our attitudes toward work, indeed our lives, change for the better if we understood that we have nothing to lose by being who we are and letting that be our compass? What better time than in our mature years to rediscover what we felt passionate about, dreamed about, loved doing, when we were young, and go forward from there? You can do it, if you are willing to make *that quest* your work for a period of time. You could warm up with the exercises below, or browse through Chapter 4, 101 Opportunities for the Open-Minded for inspiration. (Barbara Sher has some wonderful mind-openers in *It's Only Too Late If You Don't Start Now*.)

How will you know when you have found your "life's work"?

When Henry and Isabel Coryat describe their work as artisans, words like "passion" and "complete fulfillment" come up. They speak of the willingness to endure risks and to accept relatively modest material success. For Bob Griffiths, his new career as author, speaker, and teacher is part of a spiritual rebirth. For us, former publishing executive and business writer, respectively, 2young-2retire has given us a sense of mission that keeps us going when the going gets tough. It is the adventure that chose us.

Try This

To paraphrase country music icon Dolly Parton, and borrow liberally from the ancient Hindu *Bhagavad Gita*, our job is to find out who we are and "do it on purpose." To this end, each of us was born with unique abilities, gifts, and talents, eager to be expressed. Sadly, the world (our well-meaning parents, relatives and friends, schools, even the economic system under which we live) has other ideas and tries to mold us accordingly. It works, for a time. Then (happily), around our fiftieth birthday, all hell breaks loose. Call it midlife crisis if you must (we don't). Just don't miss the opportunity to begin again.

- Revisit your childhood and/or early adulthood for some clues. Set aside a few hours to tour your personal past, and like any good researcher, make careful notes in your notebook or journal. Here are a few questions to help you on your way:

  What was your happiest age or most memorable phase of life? Why? Stimulate your memory by dipping into the family album. Take your time and look for hints behind the obvious details of time and place, e.g., the expression on your face, what you were wearing, a favorite relative, or a meaningful event. This can be so much fun that you may have to remind yourself to stay on track.

What did you love doing? What did you enjoy so much it always felt like play and the time flew when you were so engaged? List your favorite activities in any order, then go back and mark the top three. In what ways do these activities show up in your life today?

Who were your friends? What did you most enjoy about them? What did they have in common?

Who was your favorite teacher, mentor, or other revered adult? Picture them. Hear their voices. What was the most memorable lesson you received from them?

- Make an inventory of your assets: natural talents, acquired skills, and so-called intangible qualities, like your optimism or sense of humor. Be bold. Include things that you might be reluctant to share in a conventional job interview.

- Make a list of every personal milestone and major accomplishment you've had throughout your life. What did you learn that has been useful throughout your life?

- Make a list of what you consider your failures or shortcomings. Reframe these as valuable life lessons and let go of the details. We could all practice a little selective amnesia in this regard.

- On one side of a page, take inventory of every bad work situation you've ever experienced. On the other side, write about what you learned from each and how you would have managed things had you been in charge. Consider this your design for your next job or enterprise.

- What would you do now if you could do anything at all? Be expansive instead of getting bogged down in practicalities—it's your dream, after all.

- What might get in the way of realizing your dreams? Exorcise those self-imposed obstacles for what they are by getting them out of your head and onto a sheet in your notebook. Expose them to the light where, like Dracula, they will vaporize. If the roadblock seems truly insurmountable, consider a different path altogether.

- Envision a community around your new endeavor; begin to imagine that you are already a part of it. Who are the people you admire most and what about them do you find most appealing?

- Make a game out of research. There is a world of information waiting to be discovered. If your computer skills need a jumpstart or buffing up, do it now. You'll need to be computer- and Internet-savvy, whatever direction you ultimately choose.

- Write a letter to yourself describing your life as you want it. Seal the letter, put it somewhere safe, and make a date to return to it in six months. Many people find that the act of writing down their desires can be a shortcut to achieving them.

- Consider hiring a personal coach to support you in setting better goals in this transition. You can find coaches easily online through www.coachville.com, the organization founded by the late Thomas Leonard, who invented the profession of coaching in the 1990s.

EXPERIMENT AND GROW

- If you aren't already, get computer literate. Seniornet is an organization that is winning awards for helping the older student to stop procrastinating and learn to love their computer. Check out the website www.seniornet.org for locations near you.

- Try Elderhostel for continuing education, travel, and enrichment. This is the mother of them all. Order a catalog, feast your eyes, and get your passport in order.

- The Learning Annex. If you live in New York City, Los Angeles, San Francisco, San Diego, or Toronto, no doubt you've seen those little dispensing boxes on your corner. This is the new face of affordable, accessible, short-course continuing education with an emphasis on personal growth (lots of the big names on the circuit) and business and career opportunities. Can't beat the price!

- Barnes and Noble is giving away courses. Before they became national booksellers, B&N was best known as the textbook capital of New York, so this free, virtual university comes as no surprise.

- Esalen (Southern California), Omega Institute (New York State), and The Open Center (New York City) are icons of the personal growth and development movement. All offer a changing annual menu of fascinating programs and speakers. Most programs are week- or weekend-long, but Esalen and Omega offer longer stay programs, scholarships, and opportunities to exchange room and board for service. Esalen Institute, in Big Sur, takes the honors for the most beautiful location imaginable.

Chapter 3. It Is Working: Volunteering Revisited

The world was not left to us by our parents. It was lent to us by our children. —AFRICAN PROVERB

We must be the change we want to see in the world. —MAHATMA GANDHI

This is the earnest work. Each of us is given only so many mornings to do it— to look around and love . . . —MARY OLIVER, "THE DEER" FROM *House of Light*

"What does a gray-haired, sixty-five-year-old, white, suburban man have in common with third grade inner-city kids, and how the devil could I help them?" That was John Gualtieri's first thought the day he turned up at the Quitman Street Community School in Newark, New Jersey, as a volunteer tutor. The former Prudential attorney had his answer not long after he met and began mentoring Tyrone Watson, a nine-year-old who had entered third grade with no reading skills. Each Wednesday over the course of the school year, Gualtieri, with his wife, Maureen McGrath, a former attorney for New York Life, showed up to lead their small, group-tutoring sessions. Over flash cards and storybooks, students and tutors bonded. By the end of the year, test scores for students in the program had improved and self-confidence soared.

This story and countless others like it are the flesh and blood behind the statistics on volunteering among mature Americans, called "this country's only increasing natural resource" by Marc Freedman, president of Civic Ventures (a national nonprofit organization dedicated to expanding the social contribution of older adults), and author of *Prime Time: How Baby Boomers Will Revolutionize Retirement and Transform America*. A new study conducted by Peter D. Hart Research Associates for Civic Ventures shows that 56 percent of Americans between the ages of fifty and seventy-five are planning to make volunteering and community service an important part of their post-career life. Although volunteering in the general population appears to be decreasing—from 55.5 percent in 1998 to 44 percent in 2000, according to an Independent Sector survey—older Americans are undeterred by the impact of the economic downturn on their savings and appear "poised to assume a leadership role in rejuvenating the nation's civic life."

So volunteering—and let's be clear that, although unpaid, it *is* work—is working. In fact, volunteer activity fills a widening gap in civic life whenever government or the private, for-profit sector does not or will not act in the public interest. Enlightened business leaders know that being good, corporate citizens has a favorable impact on their staff, customers, community, and their own bottom line. Attorneys Gualtieri and McGrath are part of the highly successful Prudential ROCS (Retirees Offering Community Service) founded in 1996 to encourage community activism among experienced former staffers—including executives, lawyers, sales representatives, office managers, and administrators. Independent of Prudential, yet supported with office and meeting space, the organization links volunteers with opportunities "they might not otherwise know about," according to

Gwendolyn Evans, former board chairperson. Programs such as this are not only great public relations for a company, but "show older workers their value doesn't end with the last paycheck," Evans said.

And speaking of bottom lines, you may be surprised to learn that volunteering—also known as the "third sector"—contributes an estimated $239.2 billion to the economy according to Independent Sector estimates, and that's without cutting jobs or degrading the environment. A measure of the importance of our pro bono contributions is that the U.S. Department of Commerce has begun to include the contribution of volunteers in calculating the economic output of the nation.

Maturity's Gift

You have no doubt read that America's social fabric is frayed and perhaps you have experienced the truth of this in your own life. Basic civic obligations like voting, even in important national elections, are ignored by the majority of citizens; test scores at public schools lag behind those of other nations in the developed world; road rage is a new, growing phenomenon on the highways. Clearly, the task of reweaving society's loose strands will be monumental, but people like us are apparently rising to the occasion in larger numbers. Remarks Marc Freedman, "What we are witnessing is the reemergence of the 'we generation.'" People who were once inspired by JFK to ask what they could do for their country "appear ready to embrace their idealism once again."

What is driving this reborn idealism? One possible answer is that maturity bestows on us a unique perspective on what our role is or could be in the community. As we emerge from years of preoccupation with career building and family life, our vision clears. We see connections that weren't so obvious before. We may develop a one-world view; on some deep level, we get the reality of environmentalist John Muir's notion that when you tug at any part of nature, you find that everything else is attached to it. We believe the reason so many of us in our fifties and older are turning from "making it" to *making it better* for all of us is simply this: We see the future in the eyes of our children—biological or otherwise—and theirs.

Many ancient texts suggest an awakened sense of responsibility is part of our evolution as human beings, one of the gifts of maturity. In Hindu philosophy, midlife brings the "householder" phase of life to a close, priming us to embrace a period of self-reflection and selfless service to others. This may be our spiritual destiny, but the timetable for adopting the role of tribal elder may also be coded in our mammalian DNA. Consider this story. In an African nature preserve, a herd of elephants was moved to a new area, a process that temporarily separated the young from their parents and other adults. Before long, caretakers noted that the isolated juveniles began to exhibit "wilding"—a form of social disintegration not unlike behaviors common in our own inner cities, where families, schools, communities, and intergenerational support systems have broken down. Similarly, William Golding's visionary novel *Lord of the Flies* is (among other things) a cautionary lesson about what can happen when the grown-ups disappear and the young are in charge.

More recently, Rabbi Zalman Schachter-Shalomi (*From Age-ing to Sage-ing: A Profound New Vision of Growing Older*) made an eloquent plea that as the "wisdom keepers" of our kind, we must embrace "an ongoing responsibility for maintaining society's well-being and safeguarding the health of our ailing planet." Says Schacter-Shalomi: "The joy of passing on wisdom to younger people not only seeds the future, but crowns an elder's life with worth and nobility." In the same vein, Theodore Roszak (*America the Wise: The Longevity Revolution and the True Wealth of Nations*) sees a world in which seasoned insights, values, and abilities play a central role in creating a more just and compassionate society. Quite contrary to the competitive, survival-of-the-fittest models touted by the voices of government and Big Business, Roszak believes the future will depend on "survival of the gentlest."

These elder values are reflected in what experts have identified as a quiet social revolution based on priorities distinctly different from the market-driven culture that has dominated American life since the Industrial Revolution. The values include "authenticity— at home, in the stores, at work, and in politics . . . support [for] women's issues in many areas of life . . . the big picture [vision] in news stories and ads," notes *Cultural Creatives: How 50 Million People Are Changing the World*, a book from authors Paul H. Ray, a macro sociologist, and his wife, psychologist Sherry Ruth Anderson, who have been studying the trend for over thirteen years. According to their research, 50 million Americans—about 25 percent of our population—have already adopted changes in worldview that sound very like those espoused by Schacter-Shalomi and Roszak.

GENERATIVITY

"What do you imagine when you picture the good that will outlive you?" asks Dan P. McAdams, a professor of psychology and human development at Northwestern University and director of the Foley Center for the Study of Lives. "Perhaps you see your children grown up and happy. Perhaps you see your students flourishing. Perhaps you see a world at peace.

"I believe that the most generative people are constantly imagining such futures. They envision a better world for themselves, their families, and their society. When you imagine the future this way, it sensitizes you to the sacredness of life on earth. The most generative people among us cherish life as if it were a beautiful infant. *(continued)*

"An African proverb says, 'The world was not left to us by our parents. It was lent to us by our children.' What survives me are the world's children, for whose sake I act today. It is as if the most generative people among us most readily envision the future's children, as if they see the baby watching them. Innocent and dependent on our own efforts of care, the future looks to each of us with hope."

From "Generativity: The New Definition of Success," in *Spirituality & Health*, fall 2001. (Quoted with permission.)

Waking the Inner Activist

What does it take to awaken your inner activist? Become curious. Get out and start talking to people in your community about what's on their minds. Talk about what concerns you. Read the local paper to take the pulse of community life. Check bulletin boards at your community center, health club, or supermarket. Find others of like mind and team up. Use Internet sources like Idealist.com and others listed in this book under Resources. Make it your job and dedicate the same energy and resources to it that you would to the search for a new career—it might lead to one in the nonprofit sector. If you think your group is too insignificant to affect change, remember Margaret Meade's often quoted words: "Never doubt that a small group of thoughtful, committed people can change the world: indeed, it's the only thing that ever has." Who knows? Maybe the people you seek are looking for you. The pro bono opportunity of your life could be around the next corner.

For much-decorated former naval officer Richard (Rick) L. Koca, Sr., father of three and grandfather of eight, the call to take action came as he watched a *48 Hours* newsmagazine segment on homeless and street kids in Southern California. It was several months before the navy transferred him to San Diego, but Koca knew that night what he was going to do when he ended his naval career. Within eight days of his arrival in California to take up his assignment, he began training to work with kids in crisis. In January 1990, with his own funds and the help of several friends, Koca founded Stand Up for Kids, an all-volunteer organization he continues to lead. Stand Up for Kids takes to the streets to rescue, educate, and involve homeless and at-risk youth—more than one and a half million children, teenagers, and young adults, based on current estimates, and 27 percent of the U.S. homeless population.

As anyone who donates their time to a worthwhile cause will tell you, volunteer work benefits giver and receiver in ways that can't be quantified. For Howard and the other mature people he recruited to Future Possibilities™, a New York City–based nonprofit organization, the hours they spend coaching inner-city schoolchildren is soul work of inestimable value. Founded by life-skills coach Lorraine White, Future Possibilities runs programs that team up adult coaches with school children, ages 7–12, in one-on-one telephone coaching sessions, KidCoach™ workshops, and after-school programs. Volunteer coaches are trained to help children discover their strengths and interests. They help them choose a goal, break it down into manageable pieces, clear hurdles, take positive risks, and celebrate success when the goal has been achieved—all things we need to be reminded of ourselves! According to White, the program is about "giving children tools to navigate the world much earlier than we had them."

Of course, as former Boy Scout leader and longtime volunteer in youth causes, Rick Koca was already primed for his personal "aha!" In Howard's case, the few hours he volunteered with the Hoboken Boys and Girls Club while he was still fully employed convinced him he wanted to work with disadvantaged children. Perhaps you, too, already have an interest—be it children, the homeless, the plight of refugees, or the environment. Follow your heart.

TOP TEN VOLUNTEER OPPORTUNITIES

Afghan Refugees are the concern of the International Rescue Committee, an organization dedicated to helping refugees settle in the United States. Volunteer at a local resettlement agency. Become an English tutor, a tour guide, or mentor to a family. www.theirc.org

CASA, an acronym for Court Appointed Special Advocate, is a national organization dedicated to homeless, abused, and neglected children. More than 900 CASA programs are in operation, with 70,000 volunteers serving 280,000 children each year. Find one in your area: http://www.nationalcasa.org/

EASI. The mission of the Environmental Alliance for Senior Involvement is to build, promote, and utilize the environmental ethic, expertise, and commitment of older people in protecting and caring for the environment for present and future generations. www.easi.org

Experience Corps® taps the experience of caring older adults in schools and youth-serving organizations to improve academic performance and development of young people. www.experiencecorps.org

Foster Grandparents is one program available in this quasi-government service site. One of the oldest of its kind. http://www.seniorcorps.org/

Habitat for Humanity International. Jimmy and Rosalind Carter are its most celebrated mature volunteers, but hundreds of people 50 and older give of their time to put roofs over those who need them, and learn a lot about construction in the process. www.habitat.org

Idealist: Action Without Borders. Founded by Ami Dar out of his experience as an Israeli paratrooper in the Lebanese war of 1982, this is one of the best international volunteer sites we've seen for bringing volunteers and opportunities together. A powerful ally for your inner activist. www.idealist.org

Stand Up for Kids. Founded by former Naval officer, Rick Koca, this nationally acclaimed volunteer organization is committed to the rescue of homeless and street kids. It is 99.5 percent volunteer run and they need help. www.standupforkids.org

The Nature Conservancy is a national nonprofit that preserves parcels of land from development by buying them and returning them to their natural state. Nature lovers, take note: volunteer opportunities are available in each state. www.nature.org

Volunteer Match is dedicated to making it easy to find volunteer opportunities wherever you live and is a partner in the recently launched USA Freedom Corps Network. http://volunteermatch.org/

For more ideas, see **Resources** section.

Quality experts, Ian Durand and his wife, April Cormaci, had built successful careers at Bell Laboratories, then launched a flourishing consultancy, traveling around the world to teach and speak about the principles of ISO 9000, a set of industrial standards used by industry around the globe. They needed to slow down to recognize what was missing in their lives. Back home in Edison, New Jersey, they turned their attention to something more heartfelt: bonding with local environmental and neighborhood groups dedicated to improving the quality of life. In 1997, using their own funds, Durand and Cormaci founded The Center for Community Renewal. The nonprofit organization makes seed-money grants to other community organizations such as the Edison Wetlands Association, Healthy Neighbors, and the local library. As two of

Edison's more visible citizens, they stop to talk with neighbors so frequently, it takes them twice as long to complete their errands around town. But that's just the way they like it.

Shimon Schwarzschild, cofounder of Action for Nature, Inc., a San Francisco—based environmental organization, decided at age ten he would one day devote his life to good causes. After a long, successful career as an electrical engineer, his childhood promise reasserted itself: "I reached a point where I felt I wanted to serve the earth rather than being a part of its destruction." He decided to take a year's leave of absence from his engineering job to accept a position as executive director of American Youth Hostels in San Francisco, despite a significant cut in pay. One year stretched into three, and his career as community activist was born. "I was having so much fun, I decided to resign from the engineering firm. I never went back." Since then, Schwarzschild has led an international campaign to save the fabled songbirds of Assisi; been director of the Whale Center in Oakland, California, working for whale protection and ocean conservation; and cofounded the Native Yew Conservation Council. (Extracts from the wild yew are used experimentally in cancer treatment.) What's ahead for this seasoned conservationist? "Right now, we want to expand by taking Action for Nature into the classroom, letting young people know how they can take personal action to protect their community's environment."

Suppose you don't have the financial resources or networks of Durand and Cormaci, Koca, or Schwarzschild to launch your own organization. Maybe you are already engaged in community service and have good ideas about how you can deepen your commitment. Wherever you find yourself in the generosity spectrum, be assured that there are 1,230,000 charities, social welfare, and faith-based organizations eager to hear from you. If, like us, you have a bias toward working with the next generation, the chances of finding a tutoring or mentoring option in a city near you are high. Experience Corps®, a program of Civic Ventures, the nonprofit organization mentioned earlier led by Marc Freedman, trains volunteers to provide tutoring, homework assistance, and other supports for children and parents. Make a commitment to serve Experience Corps® at least fifteen hours a week and receive a small stipend to cover out-of-pocket expenses. We would love to see our government sweeten its call for more volunteers with a little carrot like that. (In fact, the Civic Ventures survey cited earlier suggests that the numbers of older Americans in volunteer service would double if small incentives like enhanced prescription drug benefits were offered.) If you don't have fifteen hours a week to spare, there are also opportunities for part-time and periodic assignments. Experience Corps® was launched in Bay Area schools, and has since expanded into fifteen other cities, including New York, Washington, D.C., Boston, Minneapolis, and Portland, Oregon. A version of Experience Corps® was recently transplanted to the UK.

BACK TO SCHOOL—AS A VOLUNTEER

Tutoring: Like Prudential ROCS tutors, John Gualtieri and Maureen McGrath, you can work with students on a one-to-one basis or with small groups, concentrating on specific learning needs in reading, math, or science.

Reading buddies: Insecure about your tutoring abilities? Schools can always use volunteers to read aloud to a group of students, discuss a book, or help with vocabulary and comprehension.

Enrichment activities: Bring your special skills and talents—music, martial arts, cooking, sports, crafts, gardening, writing, or a specific country or culture—into the classroom. For maximum impact, do a demonstration.

Classroom teacher's aide: Overworked teachers can use your help in preparing and organizing class materials, checking tests, completing and collecting records, distributing materials, and working with students on special projects.

Librarian's assistant: Book lovers, this one's for you. Work in the library to help children select books, catalog books, read, tell, or tape stories, or listen to children read stories.

Computer lab assistant: Calling all computer wizards! Can you imagine anything more enjoyable than introducing young minds to the wonders of this tool?

Career education: Everything you ever learned on the job will be of interest to those looking ahead to their careers: resume writing, interviewing skills, prerequisites for hiring, and what you did and didn't like about your chosen field.

Living historians: Tom Breslauer, a Holocaust survivor, has created a fascinating talk for high school students from his personal recollections of that period. Check it out at this link: www.2young

2retire.com/breslauer.htm. You can also share your direct experience of the Civil Rights or Feminist movements or "war stories" with a new audience by becoming an interview subject.

Adapted from Intergenerational Innovations, Seattle, Washington.

Idealists in Motion

Remember when you wanted to strap on a backpack and see the world for yourself? You weren't afraid of roughing it if necessary because the adventure was worth Spartan lodgings, long waits for slow trains, and a shortage of home-cooked meals. Well, those instincts are intact, and if the time is right for you, you can combine your passion for the exotic with a desire to serve. And in many cases, volunteering your time pays your way or a significant portion of your expenses.

"Help Wanted: International business consultants needed for twenty-seven-month assignments in Russia, Eastern Europe, Africa, and Latin America." Once associated with idealistic youth, the Peace Corps is putting out a welcome mat for mature applicants, as this advertisement in *The Wall Street Journal* shows. Currently, 8 percent of Peace Corps volunteers are fifty or older, and the oldest is eighty-two. The new recruiting message aimed at mature prospects is likely to resonate with many of us: "You will have the opportunity to share a lifetime of work and wisdom with people of developing nations who respect and appreciate age. And because there's no upper age limit to serve, it's never too late—volunteers who are well into their eighties have served and continue to serve."

One of the most famous elder Peace Corps volunteers was Lillian Carter, mother of former president Jimmy Carter (who is one of this country's most famous silver-haired volunteers with Habitat

for Humanity, another organization with a global reach that at-
tracts many of us in our fifties and beyond). The newest wrinkle in
the Peace Corps to appeal to the pin-striped set is that experiences
in the developing world—helping to set up basic business systems
and even to teach English, the language of global commerce—can
actually improve one's chance for career advancement back home.
Not that most volunteers have that in mind, but the message of
"practical idealism" reflects the organizations' interest in volunteers with experience, skills, and long-range career goals. It certainly didn't hurt the prospects for prominent alumni like Donna
Shalala, former secretary of health and human services, and Robert
Haas, president of Levis Strauss.

Global Volunteers is another organization that puts the skills of
experienced professionals to use in the developing world, usually
for commitments of shorter duration. The broad goals are similar
to those of the Peace Corps: an interchange of ideas and cultures
that enable volunteers and their hosts to learn from one another.
World-travel enthusiasts Herbert and Phyllis Goldberg—a former
plastic surgeon and a marriage-and-family therapist, respectively—
are active Global Volunteers. Their first assignment took them to
Vietnam for three weeks, where they "taught conversational English, advised in the hospital and medical clinics, taught medical
and psychological policy, and the American way of life." Back at
home in California, the Drs. Goldberg are involved as volunteers in
settings that match their interests. These include teaching seminars on retirement issues at the Emeriti Center at the University of
Southern California. They want to continue to "mentor younger
adults and those approaching retirement on how to adjust, plan,
and cope." They work at local, free clinics, and do crisis intervention
for the Red Cross. For the Goldbergs, this *is* the good life.

Social Entrepreneurs

Unless a monastic lifestyle and vows of poverty are your thing, you can continue to make money while also doing good. "Social entrepreneurship," a term that may have been coined in 1991 to describe the Partnership for a Drug-Free America and other cause-driven organizations, is a hybrid of sound business practices, high ethical standards, and idealism. Today, it includes a wide variety of for-profit businesses with a social mission, of which Ben & Jerry's Ice Cream (before it was acquired by Unilever) and actor Paul Newman's food company, Newman's Own, are perhaps the most famous examples. The tongue-in-cheek motto of Newman's Own says it all: "Shameless exploitation in pursuit of the common good." Off-road attitude personified! All after-tax profits are given to causes Paul Newman believes in, typically those that address the needs of underserved segments of the population.

Ben Cohen, cofounder of Vermont's homegrown ice-cream company, Ben & Jerry's, is using his wealth and celebrity to draw attention to "unnecessary spending on Cold War–era weapons" and a variety of other progressive issues, poverty, and world hunger among them. Long associated with political activism, Cohen has launched a new organization called True Majority and attracted the support of other high-profile people like Newman and Ted Turner. Famous for starting CNN, Turner also helped bail out (and embarrass) our government with a multimillion-dollar contribution toward payment of its overdue United Nations bill. A traveling media show and an eye-catching Web site, www.truemajority.org, keep members abreast of legislation under consideration by Congress and makes it very easy to target and reach representatives with persistent e-mails and faxes on the issues. Gadflies, bookmark this URL.

Although having a household name helps fast-track these endeavors, social entrepreneurship is also flourishing for less-celebrated fifty- and sixty-somethings. In fact, there are serious outbreaks among business people like Don Schmitz, founder of intergenerational camps, and Dick Dunn, who has successfully parlayed his business associations and savvy into an event local children look forward to all year.

Schmitz, a former elementary schoolteacher and owner of a successful staffing business, was motivated by a personal experience to create a business dedicated to uniting grandparents and grandchildren. As the grandfather of three granddaughters who all now live in Sweden, he understood the challenges (and heartache) of long-distance grandparenting. Given the mobility of our society, Don Schmitz knew his experience wasn't unique. In fact, he discovered that 60 percent of grandparents live more than a day's drive away from their grandchildren. After completing an advanced degree in human development, he founded www.Grandkidsandme.com, an organization that uses two main avenues to carry out Schmitz's vision of successful grandparenting: Grandparent Groups and Grandparent Camps, both designed to help grandparents focus on their important role, and his own growing role as a public speaker on the subject. After he caught the attention of *The Wall Street Journal*, Schmitz has had no difficulty filling up those bunk beds.

Dick Dunn made his mark in managed care in North Carolina, and is still involved in the health-insurance industry. But the former HMO executive has another project that evolved from and is nurtured by his business associations. It began when he became involved in the local Salvation Army Christmas Bureau, which sets up a "toyland" for the needy parents to "shop" for their children at no cost. The friend who had brought him into this program challenged

Dunn to raise money for bicycles to give away with the other toys. Today, Dunn and his business colleagues run The Spokesgroup, a nonprofit dedicated to providing bicycles to disadvantaged children. Their goal is to provide bicycles to every child who wants one. Their Web site is www.thespokesgroup.com. Good for the community, and not bad for Dunn's insurance business either.

"How we decide to behave as elders will be the most important challenge we face," writes Ken Dychtwald in *Age Wave: How the Most Important Trend of Our Time Will Change Our Future*. Many of us fifty and older have decided we will *be the change* we want to see in the world. Whatever calls to us; however we go about it; however long it takes to see positive results from our efforts, our numbers ensure we can be an unprecedented force for good.

Try This

What can you do if you don't have the motivation or wherewithal to start a foundation? Are you going to be stuck stuffing envelopes? Not necessarily (although in an organization you are interested in, it's not a bad way to be a fly on the wall). One of the advantages of pro bono work is the smorgasbord of opportunities available to you and the unparalleled chance to try out new things. Besides, social activism takes practice, so don't be afraid to take the plunge.

- Today, perform one random, unsolicited act of generosity or kindness. It can be as simple as taking a trash bag along on your walk and picking up litter, or calling the local nursing home to offer your services as a reader for an hour or so. Jot down in your journal or notebook how this felt, and where in your body you felt it.

- Think back: whose selfless service made a difference in your own life—parents, grandparents, a special teacher, coach, mentor, friend, or stranger? Draft a letter of appreciation in your notebook, and consider sending the letter.

- Study your annual charitable giving. Was it the organization's persistence that got you to write a check or something more important: an inner resonance with its goals? What do you know about these organizations? Narrow the field and go deep. This could be the door to your next volunteer opportunity or nonprofit career.

- When television was in its formative years, there was an irresistible program called *The Millionaire* in which a wealthy donor gave a needy person financial security for life. Well, inflation aside, a million dollars is still a lot of money. Imagine you have $1,000,000 to give away. How or to whom would you distribute it. Why?

- Imagine you have no money for charity. What will you contribute instead that is uniquely yours? Make a list.

- What about your town (city, country, world) stirs your civic consciousness or makes you angry? Why? If you ruled the world, what changes would you make? Write them down in a journal or notebook.

- Draft a letter to the editor of your local paper describing a problem in your community and proposing a solution. Let your passion show.

- Compose a letter to your representative in Washington (or the president) about something you believe needs urgent attention. Make suggestions. Follow up by phone, fax, or e-mail. Remember, they are on *your* payroll.

- Describe your ideal world to a grandchild (yours or someone else's). What one small step can you take toward achieving that vision? Make a plan and follow through.

Chapter 4.
101 Opportunities
for the Open-Minded

Life is a perpetual instruction in cause and effect.
　　　　　　　　—RALPH WALDO EMERSON

Creative thinking may mean simply the realization that there's no particular virtue in doing things the way they have always been done. —RUDOLPH FLESCH
　　　　(AUTHOR, COMMUNICATION SKILLS GURU)

I miss 100% of the shots I never take.
　　　　　　—WAYNE GRETZKY, ICE HOCKEY SUPERSTAR

Chief Energizer Officer
Chief Humor Officer
Creatologist
Director, Department of the Future
Ethicist
Left Brain
Outside General Counsel
VP Cool

You won't find these job titles in the U.S. Department of Labor's *Dictionary of Occupational Titles*, but that doesn't mean they don't or couldn't exist. In the late twentieth century, new jobs were created faster than we could categorize them, suggesting the creation of useful work and ways of working is limited only by our imagination. Human creativity proves again that it can take on just about anything the times dish out. Fortunately for all of us, imagination is something *Homo sapiens* were born with and it is ageless. The ability to see more than is evident separates us from every other being, except possibly our primate brethren, the chimpanzee, which took a few million millennia to develop rudimentary tools.

Imagination, as you probably know, never moves in a straight line. It takes you on a zigzag course. In pursuit of your bliss, you leap, you soar, you land in places you hadn't anticipated. In fact, the power of imagination is its unpredictability, the happy accidents that occur when someone is going about their life, but happens to be in the right place, at the right time. Just ask any inventor. You might examine the circuitous route taken by many people to successful second, even third, careers, in the True Stories profiles in www.2young2retire.com. A county-court judge who became an elementary schoolteacher. A Wall Streeter who morphed into an author and motivational speaker. The phone installer who launched herself as a senior life-skills trainer. Not only doable, *done*.

Like any other inborn talent, imagination needs to be cultivated and encouraged. If you've been in a job that didn't reward an entrepreneurial spirit let alone sideways thinking, now may be your chance to give that genius free rein. Prepare to move that big brain of yours up, down, and sideways as you consider the following list of 101 opportunities. Let it be a springboard to inventions of your own.

Don't expect any "Make $5,000 a month working from home" claims here. Maybe there is some truth to them, but we're here to steer you toward more solid, proven opportunities to make money. Each listing is followed by a symbol: the sun ☼ is for jobs that can yield at least a comfortable middle-class income ($30–50K) when pursued with full-time commitment; the moon ☾ for work that can supplement income (and/or is fulfilling in other ways). A number of these opportunities can start out part-time then become the whole enchilada; it's up to you.

Think Like an Entrepreneur

If you became a butcher, baker, or candlestick maker because that's what you always wanted to be, you are in the minority. Many of us find ourselves in a career without fully understanding how it happened to us. We needed to make a living, of course, but we may also have been influenced by family pressure, issues of self-esteem, or what the guidance counselor said. Richard Bolles's revolutionary book *What Color Is Your Parachute?* remains the Bible of career change, now in its umpteenth edition (see Resources). Now is the time to map out your dream job and to explore possibilities that your radar might not have detected. Career experts today say it's far healthier to be *continuously* thinking about the next job or opportunity than waiting for the other shoe to drop. So do yourself a favor and begin to research your next move, even if you are still happily employed. Become an entrepreneur about *you*. Trust us: procrastination takes at least as much hard work as action.

Ready? Here we go.

Ageless Adventurer to Yoga Teacher

1. **Ageless adventurer.** Answer the call of the wild. Work on a riverboat and satisfy your inner Huckleberry Finn. RiverBarge Excursion Lines, Inc. http://www.riverbarge.com/, 888-256-7573 or peopledepartment@riverbarge.com. ☼
2. **Animal handler.** It runs the gamut from biological fieldwork

to public speaking and education to cleaning out the cage or tank, but if you love a particular species, e.g., dolphins or parrots, and want to work with them, get the straight story from this Web site: http://www.arkanimals.com/Career/Career1.html. ☼

3. **Antique restorer.** If you have an itch to preserve the past and some handyperson skills, this is a low-investment business that can earn you a handsome payback. Scour the flea markets for some junk you can practice on. ☾

4. **Artisan apprentice.** A couple we know dropped out of a glamorous lifestyle—he was an international banker, she a gallery owner—to reinvent themselves as artisans. For a year they apprenticed themselves to a bronze-casting atelier and emerged to launch their own business. See the Coryats's story, Chapter 2, visit their Web site (www.coryatcasting.com), or contact them directly: hicoryat@valstar.net. ☼

5. **Astrologer.** They may not admit it, but many people won't make a move without consulting an astrologer. If this is your passion, you can develop a healthy practice among the star-struck. The American Federation of Astrologers has a home study course and other information : http://www.astrologers. com/. ☾ ☼

6. **Author.** This perennially cool career has gotten a lot easier with the explosion in self-publishing opportunities, in-cluding print-on-demand and downloadable e-books. Now you can take your work directly to an audience at relatively low cost by cutting out all those middle people. The mar-keting was always up to you anyway, unless you were so well-known you didn't really need it. Take advantage of the level playing field. Check out www.greatunpublished.com, www.1stbooks.com, and www.xlibris.com among others. Read the fine print before you sign up. ☾ ☼

7. **Baby or kid wrangler.** Someone has to manage those adorable children you see in print advertising or commercials. A natural for anyone with professional preschool or elementary-school teaching credentials, not to mention experienced grandparents. ☼

8. **Bed and breakfast host.** Got a charming and/or conveniently located home? You can make some extra money renting out a portion of it to visitors who prefer a home to a hotel. In some cities, you can register with a bureau that specializes in hooking up B&B hosts with prospects. Get a flavor for this at: www.manhattangetaways.com or www.nyhabitat.com. If you can make it there ... ☾

9. **Bike messenger.** Build up your quads while you deliver those messages and packages around town. Get yourself bonded to handle sensitive documents and a bicycle that is light enough to be stowed easily in a safe place while you call on customers. Insure it and you, of course. ☼

10. **Board game inventor.** Were you reared on Monopoly? Let your imagination be your laboratory for the next, big, board-game craze. A not so trivial pursuit. ☾

11. **Book or script doctor.** You can earn between $50–75 messing with someone else's deathless prose to make it more marketable. Do a little guerrilla research by checking out the reader reviews on www.Amazon.com. A good way to spot trends. ☼

12. **Booking agent.** Passionate about dance or musical troupes? Help them find an audience by providing this valuable service. A neighbor of ours ran a booking service for three dance companies and made good money at it, for her protégés and herself. ☾ ☼

13. **Business-plan writer.** Many software packages can help you structure a business plan. But helping those with a great idea

who are clueless about how to conceptualize it on paper means tapping into your own experience and business savvy. That puts you ahead of plain-vanilla plans. ☼

14. **Cabaret singer.** Like many opportunities to perform, you have to be willing to give it away free to get your start. Put together a CD of your favorite songs and make the rounds—your local parks department, community centers, hospitals—you get the idea. Exposure, exposure, exposure. ☾

15. **Cake decorator.** Are you an artist with icing sugar? You can start a specialty cake business with your imagination and a small investment in equipment and tools. Demonstrate in the kitchenware department of your favorite store or promote yourself through workshops. ☾

16. **Caretaker.** Professional house sitters (aka property managers) get free board and sometimes even a salary and health-care insurance. Gary Dunn's newsletter, *The Caretaker Gazette*, lists opportunities six times a year. To subscribe or browse, check the Web site www.caretaker.org. ☾

17. **Celebrity impersonator.** Elvis look-alikes are so numerous they have an annual convention. But suppose you resemble Bill Clinton, Jerry Seinfeld, or Oprah enough to launch a spate of "separated at birth" jokes? Convention and meeting planners could be looking for you to add some spice to the proceedings. ☾

18. **Club Med G.O.**, that's *Gentile Organisateur* (aka staff), those friendly, enthusiastic folks in sarongs who teach everything from aerobics to water-skiing at Villages around the world. The "swinging single" image is history and families and mature *Gentile Membres* (guests) are in. ☼

19. **Clown** for children's parties. Been to any birthday parties at Chuck E. Cheese's? Maybe you don't have the electronic bells

and whistles, but if you have a flair for performing and love little children, you can outdo the entertainment with one hand
tied behind your back. Probably safer than joining the circus,
too. ☾

20. **Companion service.** All the lonely people are not in the sin-
gles column of your local paper. Some of them are elderly,
shut-in, and physically challenged. Match them up with
screened, caring companions for a fee. Do good; do well. ☾

21. **Composer** of original songs, poems, speeches for family and
school reunions, special birthdays, weddings, etc. One guy we
know has created templates into which he plugs the salient
information. You don't have to be a Rogers and Hammerstein
to make your audience go dewy-eyed. This is a captive audience in the best sense of the word. ☾

22. **Computer tutor.** Are you Word Perfect? Do you Excel? The
numbers of small businesses who need computer training
like *yesterday* keeps growing. Going rate is $50/hour mini-
mum. ☼

23. **Craft instructor.** Interest in crafts is exploding. A family of
quilt enthusiasts converted a barn on their rural property into
a quilt museum, where they gave workshops and sold supplies. ☾

24. **Croupier.** Casinos, many of them Native American run, are
popping up in lots of places. Unlike most casino clients, a
skilled blackjack dealer can make a good buck. Thrills without
personal risk. ☼

25. **Cruise ship lecturer.** So much downtime between ports. So
many opportunities to blow your diet. No wonder professors
and other experts with presentation skills are in demand on
the cruise-line circuit. Not a bad idea for aerobic instructors,
musicians, and yoga teachers with a little wanderlust, either. ☾

26. **Customized greeting card designer.** Create customized greeting cards using your creativity and desktop publishing skills. Sure, there's Blue Mountain e-cards, but these one-of-a-kind cards that get delivered by snail mail count for more. How about wedding and special anniversary invitations? You moonlighting calligraphers, take note. ☾

27. **Declutter coach.** Okay, personal organizer. You hate chaos and love order. This could be the career for you. Check out what others with a similar interest are doing and plot your own move. National Association of Professional Organizers: www.napo.net and http://dmoz.org/Home/Personal__ Organization/Consultants/. Also check out Professional organizers Web ring, www.organizeswebring.com.

28. **Desktop publishing for small business.** Got Mac or computer-graphics skills and an eye for design? Small businesses need all the help they can get to communicate more vibrantly to prospective clients. See also Computer Tutor above, and double the hourly rate. ☼

29. **Dog-walking service.** A dog-loving neighbor of ours has carved out a thriving little business for herself taking dogs out for their daily constitutional and charging the owners a monthly fee that makes baby-sitting pale by comparison. Not a bad way to stay fit and trim, either. ☼

30. **Doula.** Here's a growing profession that helps women through labor and childbirth, using nonmedical interventions like breathing techniques, massage, aromatherapy, and masses of emotional support. Membership in the Doulas of North America association has grown from eighty-five in 1992 to three thousand, according to *Cool Careers for Dummies*. Visit www.dona.com for more information. ☼

31. **Dream analyst.** A dream job. You might use your skill in interpreting the narrative, images, and symbols of dreams for entertainment purposes. Or, if you believe that dreams have meaning and purpose, you might help others tap theirs for ideas, inspiration, and insights. Here's more information: http://www.dreamanalysis.info/faqs.html. ℂ

32. **Drive/deliver cars** for an auto-rental agency. It's not the Indianapolis 500, but if you enjoy driving, have a current driver's license, and a clean safety record, this is a good way to see the country all expenses paid. ℂ

33. **eBay expert.** Turn your obsession with this Web-based answer to consumer excess to your own advantage. Teach others the ropes, share your tips in a specialized newsletter, or offer counseling to the auction-addicted. ℂ

34. **English as a second language (ESL) and English as a foreign language (EFL) teachers** are in demand both in the United States and around the world. A good career for the stay-at-home, but you can also satisfy your wanderlust and share your native tongue with those hungry to learn it. National Clearinghouse for ESL Literacy Education: www.cal.org/ncle, http://www.eslemployment.com/. See also, Dave's ESLCafe's Web guide, www.eslcafe.com. ☼

35. **Executive chef.** No, not those glamorous types you see on cable or the harried hash-slingers in the institutional kitchen. We mean the professionals who work normal hours—never or rarely on weekends—creating interesting dishes for the executive dining room. Develop a specialty, for example natural foods, and market yourself to spas or specialty cruise lines. ☼

36. **Expert witness.** Perhaps you have some job experience that could make you invaluable as an expert witness in disputes,

hearings, or legal proceedings. Our sister-in-law was a disability claims examiner for decades. After she retired from that career, her expertise made her much in demand in disputed claims. ☾

37. **Family business consultant.** A specialized field but a well-paid one for those who want to help family businesses—a larger segment than you might realize—function better and handle succession issues. More information from The Family Firm Institute, www.ffi.org. ☼

38. **Farmer or rancher.** Maybe you can grow baby vegetables and herbs for a farmer's market, or, if your love of wildlife includes the animal variety, perhaps alpaca ranching is more your line. Alpaca Owners and Breeders Association (United States) 1-800-213-9522, www.aoba.org, or read about a couple who are doing it, www.2young2retire.com/bellizzi.html. ☼

39. **Fee-based financial planner.** Maturity is an advantage in this growing field, which is part therapist, part investment adviser. If you like working with people and numbers, this could be up your alley. See Certified Financial Planner Board of Standards, Inc., www.cfp.net. Also check the National Association of Personal Financial Advisers for fee-only (as opposed to commission-based compensation) practitioners. www.napfa.org. ☼

40. **Flight attendant.** The major airlines are recruiting. You need good health, communications skills, a desire to work with the public, and the ability to learn and perform flight-safety basics. Nice travel benefits for you and your family, too. Personally, we love seeing mature faces in the aisles. ☼

41. **Food cooperative manager.** A grass-roots business in which members do most of the work, food cooperatives bring organic

vegetables and other products to suburban and urban dwellers. A musician we know started this in her community as a side to her main pursuit and has since expanded it countywide. ☾

42. **Franchises.** The upside: buying into a ready-made business can reduce some of the risks. The downside: It can be costly. But exploring franchise opportunities can be a great way to research for a business niche that isn't overexploited and get a handle on typical start-up costs. Visit: http://www.franchisecentral.com for a sampling of what's hot right now. ☼

43. **Freelance floral or gift-basket designer.** Pure creativity with a dash of marketing genius can launch this interesting profession. Wedding specialists have been known to jet to exotic locales for celebrity weddings. ☼ ☾

44. **Garage sale organizer** (also estate and moving sales). If you are someone who brakes for garages sales, you might turn this passion into the local equivalent of eBay, and take a cut of the proceeds. Civic minded? Donate part of your take to a local charity. Your investment: an advertisement in *Penny Saver* and some business cards. ☾

45. **Ghostwriter.** Sure, your name may not appear on the book itself until you get better known, and then only following the "with." But if you love to write and are a quick study of others' interest, this could be a well-paid opportunity. Check out this site for ideas: www.publishersmarketplace.com. ☼

46. **Good news newsletter.** Sick of the daily headlines? You can do something about adjusting everyone's attitude in a positive direction with your own newsletter or column. Good writing and computer skills a must. Visit the Newsletter and Electronic Publishers Association for more how-to information: www.newsletters.org. ☼

47. **Green market organizer.** Blend your love of fresh produce,

cheese, and other products from small farmers with your organizational savvy. Most communities you'd want to live in will support a green market. And you can collect some fees for providing this valuable service. Visit a green market for ideas, contacts, and lettuce that tastes like lettuce. ☾

48. **Hairstylist to go.** Doctors may not make house calls anymore, but you can. Get a regular gig at the assisted-living facility. Sell your services to schools and hospitals. You're building morale, not just a new "do." ☾

49. **Historian.** A man we know got a grant to write a history of his hometown. Another—an amateur photographer—is being paid to create a photo essay of his. Check out your library and see who has done what and how you can improve on it. ☾

50. **Home cleaning service.** It's the homework that never ends and many people are willing to turn it over to professionals. In our town, the guy who started one of these now has a fleet of vans that deliver cheerful, efficient cleaners to your door on a weekly or twice-a-month schedule. His home, presumably spotless, has a water view. ☼

51. **Home finder specialist.** You work with the client on their requirement, e.g., an artist seeking a live/work studio; a special-needs family seeking compatible housing; elders wanting to sort through assisted living options. Then bring them together with realtors for a fee. ☾

52. **Hypnotherapist.** Smoking. Overeating. Shopaholism. As long as there are addictions like these, there will be plenty of work for hypnotherapists, a growing area of the mental-health profession. For more about the subject, read http://www.natboard.com/essay.html. Other sources, The National Guild of Hypnotherapists: http://www.ngh.net/ and the American Association of Professional Hypnotherapists, http://aaph.org/. ☼

53. **Inventor.** If necessity is the mother of invention, a passion for problem solving must be its father. Think for a moment about the numbers of tools now available to remove the paper husk from garlic; the variety of self-cleaning presses to get that essential ingredient into a recipe. Do the words "patent pending" make your heart beat faster? Check out these sites: http://inventors.about.com/; http://www.enchantedlearning.com/inventors/. ☼ ☾

54. **Karaoke DJ.** Turn your love for people and disco music into a career and party *down* as many nights as you want to. Karaoke hosts can make between $30–55K a year and you don't need any formal education. ☼

55. **Laughter therapist.** Children laugh somewhere on the order of forty times a day. Adults maybe ten. Phyllis Popkin, a former elementary schoolteacher, decided to get in touch with her inner comedienne and turn it into a career. Reinventing herself as The Laughter Lady, she now brings humor into the workplace, to conferences, and other venues for a fee. ☾

56. **Letter-writing service** for non-English speakers. From getting a foot in the door for a desired job to settling disputes without legal expenses, a literate letter can make all the difference. Think about trying to explain something complicated in a language not your own, and you'll get a sense of the value of this service. Good for buffing up your own language skills, too. ☾

57. **Market researcher.** Your natural curiosity and way with words are major assets for this cutting-edge profession. Market yourself to a polling organization. Check out Marketing Research Association, www.mra-net.org. ☼

58. **Massage therapist.** A growing profession with much job satisfaction. In most states, you need five hundred hours of

training to be licensed. Be sure your program is accredited by the Commission on Massage Training. Chair massages with the client fully clothed have proliferated in suburban malls and parks, bringing massage into the mainstream. Physical fitness is paramount because practitioners are on their feet all day. Massage Therapy Association: www.amtamassage.org. ☼

59. **Meditation instructor.** If you have discovered the benefits of meditation for yourself, you can learn to instruct others in the technique. Teach a course at your local adult school in stress management using meditation and branch out from there. ☼

60. **Microbrew operator.** Remember that Ben and Jerry's started with a correspondence course in ice-cream making, so if you have a passion for the suds and the patience to experiment (and taste) until you get something worth trumpeting, this could be for you. Check out the American Brewers Guild: http://www.abgbrew.com/. ☾

61. **Mobile dry-cleaning/shoe repair/delivery service** for home and businesses. The busier people get, the more they are willing to pay others to perform essential services. You need a reliable van, good insurance, excellent record-keeping software, and some stamina. ☼

62. **Monogramming service.** The more "high tech" we become, the more we want that personal touch. We buy our baby gifts from a woman who monograms the newborn's name on burp cloths or other necessities for a special, personalized gift. She has all the work she wants, and it all comes from referrals. ☾

63. **Motivational speaker.** Find out if this is for you by joining your local Toastmasters group. http://www.toastmasters.org. Also check out some speaking websites to get a flavor of this exciting career, here's one: http://www.speaking.com/. Develop a specialty and practice what you preach. ☼

64. **Movie extra.** Insiders say it's not that difficult to break into, but the work can be tedious with much waiting around, so patience, a sense of humor, and a good book are mandatory. You have to register with Central Casting (yes, there is one) in Los Angeles, (www.entertainmentpartners.com/products_and_services/services/central_casting/) and check out the trade papers: *The Reporter, Variety, Drama Logue* all have jobs listed. Also check out 411, the industry book, available at the Samuel French Bookstore on Laurel Canyon in Studio City. ☾

65. **Moviemaker.** Maybe your claim to fame was acceptance in America's Funniest Home Videos. But these days, anyone with a compact video cam and a sharp eye can play. Maybe there's a great idea for a documentary or the next breakthrough "indie" waiting to be discovered. Visit: http://www.cyberfilmschool.com/. ☼

66. **Nanny.** Until your own grandchildren show up, you could be making a respectable living (taking into account that room and board often comes with it) looking after other people's offspring. For training and a good source of referrals, check American Council of Nanny Schools, 517-686-9470. International Nanny Association, www.nanny.org, publishes a directory of nanny-training programs. ☼

67. **Navy teacher.** Central Texas College has a contract to provide teachers to the navy. Check their Web site, www.ctcd.cc.tx.us, or write to PACE Program, Central Texas College, 6200 West Central Texas Expressway, P.O. Box 1800, Killeen, Texas 76540. (See Ann Mariah Stewart, Chapter 2.) ☼

68. **Park ranger or wildlife guide.** If you love the outdoors, these seasonal gigs could be right up your alley. Get acquainted with the National Park Service and you could be on their wanted list for work for many seasons to come. ☾

69. **Personal coach.** Celebrity coaches like Cheryl Richardson have put this new profession on the map. Not to be confused with therapy, coaching helps motivated people set goals and make moves in their lives they might not consider without support. A career in which life experience and maturity are major assets. Six-figure incomes are not impossible. Lots of training available. See www.coachville.com, www.coachu.com, and www.coachfederation.org for courses and other resources. ☼

70. **Personal trainer.** Create a niche, for example, mature bodies, special needs. Get certified to build, shape, and sculpt. Two resources to check out: NFPT Personal Trainer and Certification and Fitness Education, http://www.nfpt.com/, and Ace Fitness, http://www.acefitness.org/. ☼

71. **Pet sitter.** If you have any doubts about the size of this market, take a look at the grocery shelves next time you are shopping. Larger than the baby-food section, right? Check out the National Association of Profession Pet Sitters, www.petsitters.org, for more ideas. ☾

72. **Piano tuner.** According to the U.S. Department of Labor Statistics, the busiest piano tuners can potentially earn good incomes. $65–75 per hour is the going rate. An almanac on career opportunities listed piano tuners in the top twenty professions out of two hundred. Information about a piano-tuning course: http://www.pianotuningcourse.com/. ☼

73. **Playground designer.** Play is the work of children. Imagine what a great playground can do for little minds and bodies, and start sketching. Also tree house designer. ☾ ☼

74. **Product tester.** Just as it suggests, you get first shot at a product before it is ready for market. In fact, your opinion

could be the deciding factor. Heady stuff, that power. A big responsibility. ☼

75. **Professional researcher.** Love to surf the Web or the library stacks for little known facts? Name a price for your obsession and market it to authors, e-zines, or Web sites hungry for content. ☼

76. **Relocation specialist.** Find out everything there is to know about a particular city or region of interest to a would-be resident, and market yourself to the large real estate chains and the local chamber of commerce. Americans are perhaps the most "moving" people on earth, so your client-base will be replenished regularly. Employee Relocation Council: www.erc.org ☼

77. **Rent-a-husband.** Those "honey-do" jobs may not be worth hiring a contractor for, but they are right up the alley of the handyman (or woman) who can translate his or her "do-it-yourself" skills into "do-it-for-them" jobs. ☾

78. **Retailing.** A booth, cart, or kiosk of your own. Wear comfortable shoes and enjoy the great people watching. A woman we know launched a hot-dog stand at her local mall, then based on customer enthusiasm, scaled-up her old family recipe for relish into a branded product. (See Anne Kleine, Chapter 2.) ☼

79. **Repair bicycles** (watches, old clocks, computers, VCRs). Many people are tired of our "disposable" mind-set and want to extend the life of the stuff they already have. If you're handy with the above mentioned or other staples of modern life, you could convert your skills into cash. ☾

80. **Resume-writing service.** "Getting" someone down on a sheet or two for a prospective employer is an art form. Making them stand out from the crowd is a marketing skill. If you can

do both and are naturally curious about people, this is an easy, low-cost business to launch. ☾

81. **Reunion organizer.** Families and former classmates are pulling together once again, but not everyone has the time or talent to organize a reunion on a large scale. Like your colleagues, the event or wedding planner, a cool head, a fat Rolodex of contacts, and a warm personality can take you far. National Association of Reunion Managers: www.reunions.com. ☾

82. **Second-home, property-management business.** Off-season, the condos are shuttered, unoccupied. It doesn't take much imagination to grasp how disastrous a leak or power outage could be. Enter the property manager, who pops in for ten or fifteen minutes a week, flushes the toilets, props up the vine the wind blew down, makes sure the AC or heat is working, and nips potential problems in the bud—services owners are only too glad to pay. You might have to live in or near a resort, darn it. ☼

83. **Shopping service.** If retail therapy is your thing, here's an opportunity to express yourself without blowing a hole in your own budget. Many people need someone to shop for them, everything from groceries for shut-ins to gifts for busy executives. ☾

84. **Speech writer.** You could have said it better? Well, maybe you can and get paid handsomely to put words into someone else's mouth. Think of all those graduation addresses every year. This writer used to charge $3,500 and north for penning executive speeches. ☼

85. **Stand-up comic.** If you're naturally gregarious, love performing, and have the gift of making people laugh, you can hone it—and get exposure—at urban and suburban comedy clubs. Don't quit your day job just yet. ☾

86. **Storyteller.** A tradition that's finding new purpose today. If you are the sort of person who can keep a room spellbound, this might be for you. Storytelling conferences occur every year around the country, so find one and go listen up. http://www.storytellingfestival.net/. For more, visit http://www.story net.org/ and click on "getting started." ☾ ☼

87. **Square-dance caller.** Love this traditional form of group dance? You have plenty of company. Check out http://www.dosado.com/default.htm, for a brief history of this art form and links to "caller's colleges" around the country. ☾

88. **Home tutor.** People need tutors for all kinds of reasons, and after school or work is best for most. Making house calls will give you a competitive edge. Patience and people skills, including the ability to communicate well, are as important as knowledge of the subject matter. ☾ ☼

89. **Survey designer.** Curious marketers want to know what makes us tick. Find a niche, create an original way to ask questions, and employ one of several fully automated survey sites to deliver your products, Zoomerang for one, www.zoomerang.com. ☾

90. **Technology troubleshooter.** So many tools and toys, and manuals not worth the paper they're printed on. What's your expertise? Software installation? Computer tips and shortcuts? VCRs and DVD players? You could be a hero in no time flat. Ka-ching! ☼

91. **Tool exchange.** What's the point in everyone owning a power washer, extension ladder, document shredder, and other occasionally used tools? Create an exchange service and charge a fee for putting people and the tool they need together. ☾

92. **Tour guide #1.** Got some interesting historic or natural sights in your town? Create a walking/biking/driving tour

service for visitors. Your local chamber of commerce is a good place to start checking this out. ☾

93. **Tour guide #2.** Use your second-language skills to market tours (see above) to non-English speaking visitors. Team up with a travel agency. ☾

94. **Toy reseller.** Children get bored with toys long before they are "used-up." Provide a service by recycling good, used toys and become a local hero to thrifty parents and their children. Look at clothing consignment shops for a good model on how to operate. ☾

95. **Travel writer.** Take a page out of *Lonely Planet* and *Rough Guides* and write about experiences you won't find in the up-scale glossies. There's an audience out there with a thirst for the quirky and offbeat in travel, the unusual and rare in one's own backyard. ☾ ☼

96. **Trend spotter.** Oh, the fickleness of the consumer. If you love soaking up the culture and making predictions about the new, new thing, this line of work could be the ticket. Hey, it made a household name (almost) out of Faith Popcorn of *The Popcorn Report*. ☾

97. **Video biographer.** Wedding videos have become standard issue. But here's an opportunity to capture someone's family—especially the elders—for posterity. A compact video cam, a well-thought out interview script, and willing subjects are all you need. Team up with a reunion organizer. ☾

98. **Virtual assistants** (VAs) "are independent contractors who provide administrative support or specialized business services from a distance, through the Internet, fax, telephone, or another method of communication. They can help a company that needs extra people to meet seasonal demands; provide

unique skills for a special project; or step in to meet the demands of business growth, locally, domestically, or globally." See International Virtual Assistant Association www.ivaa.org for more general information. To find out about actual jobs, see http://www.virtualassistants.com/. ☼

99. **Wedding or event planner.** If you can keep a cool head while all around you are losing theirs, this could be your line of work. Good organizational and negotiating skills a must. Overstuffed Rolodex of useful contacts a plus. ☼

100. **Work for your children.** Got offspring with a great idea and not much cash? Give them a hand, like Ray and Marian Brovero of Royal Palm Beach, Florida, did for their chef son. The family affair is thriving. ☾

101. **Yoga teacher.** Yoga is hot! You can get a two hundred-hour certification in the evenings and weekends. Start your search with *Yoga Journal Magazine* or log on to www.yoga site.com. One of the best and most respected schools in the country is at Kripalu Center for Yoga and Health, www. kripalu.org. ☼

Try This

There's nothing so entrapping as a long career, whether it is fulfilling or not. The hours add up; they work their way into your blood. What follows are some out-of-the-box tasks to open up a space in your head. Approach this with buoyancy and a spirit of fun. What can they do to you?

- The Best Job I Never Had. Read through the 101 Opportunities again and see if it sparks anything. Start a new section called Dream Job and write about the job or business you've always wanted, but didn't dare to hope for until now. Flesh out the details, the who, what, when, where, how, as much as you can. Write without stopping, editing, or revising until you run out of things to include. Free-writing is a technique that works magic. The goal isn't perfect prose or eloquence, but truth. Don't worry. You're not obliged to share this with anyone. (If you come up with a brand-new job or business idea, feel free to please drop us a line: Howard@2young2retire.com.)

- Where in your life are you already giving expression to some elements of your dream job or ideal business? Spread a wide net and don't get hung up on whether you're getting paid for your labor. What you're after is something you can build on, no matter how small or insignificant it might seem at first.

- What one step can you take in the next week to explore your dream opportunity more fully or move it along toward reality? It doesn't have to be much more than a phone call, half an hour surfing the Internet, or an hour at the library. Whatever it is, make a commitment to carry it out and don't let yourself down.

- Create a business card for the career/business of your choice. Use the Word or Word Perfect template and some clip art for the card, then print a couple of sheets on Avery 8371 cards you can get at any office-supply place. Making your dream concrete, in even a small way, can make it feel almost inevitable.

- For the next month, set some time aside to live as if that dream opportunity was already a reality. What do you notice about yourself, about your current work, about the way others behave toward you? Keep notes on any changes you observe. You are on your way.

- Need to remain where you are while you plot your next move? Make a list of legitimate requests that could improve your current working conditions. People tend to respond better to requests than complaints.

Chapter 5.
Toward Wellness

If I knew I'd live this long, I'd have taken better care of myself.
—EUBIE BLAKE, JAZZ IMMORTAL

Of all the self-fulfilling prophecies in our culture, the assumption that aging means decline and poor health is probably the deadliest.
—MARILYN FERGUSON,
The Aquarian Conspiracy

The best prescription is knowledge.
—DR. C. EVERETT KOOP,
FORMER SURGEON GENERAL

Pop quiz. 1. Why is flossing your teeth good for your health?

(a) It helps prevent gum disease
(b) It helps prevent the formation of artery-clogging plaque
(c) It prevents bad breath, which improves your social life
(d) All the above

If you checked (d), you are right. If you are already acting on this information, you are on your way to better health and a longer life, according to the Life Expectancy Calculator® created by Thomas T.

Perls, M.D., and associates, authors of *Living to 100: Lessons in Living to Your Maximum Potential at Any Age*.

It's no secret the human life span is lengthening. Researchers Jim Oeppen of Cambridge University and James W. Vaupel of the Max Planck Institute for Demographic Research in Germany believe we will continue to break longevity records, and that the average life expectancy will reach one hundred within the next fifty years.

That is good news for us, our families, communities, countries, and the planet itself, *provided* our life span equals our health span. And that depends less on inheriting Methuselah genes or having access to the latest advances in treatment or drugs, than on making informed choices about healthy living whatever our age (the sooner, the better).

In their bestselling *The Okinawa Program*, Bradley J. Willcox, M.D., Craig Willcox, Ph.D., and Makoto Suzuki, M.D., spell out what makes Okinawans healthy throughout their long lives: a diet rich in soy products and vegetables; regular exercise; low levels of stress; and a high degree of spirituality. The New England Centenarian Study conducted by Boston's Beth Israel Deaconess Medical Center and Harvard Medical School (on which *Living to 100* was based) also pointed to lifestyle choices as the deciding factor: "Rather than the mistaken perception that 'the older you get the sicker you get,' centenarians teach us the older you get the healthier you've been." Quality of life, it turns out, can improve quantity of life.

Like centenarian jazz great Eubie Blake, we believe that when we make a conscious choice to take better care of ourselves, that alone tips the scales in our favor. Luckily for us, the wealth of information readily available makes it easy to be active participants in our own well-being. So empower yourself. Do your own research. Question authority.

Prevention Magazine and *Men's Health Magazine* are just two resources as near as your newsstand. Popular health writers like columnist Jane Brody of *The New York Times* regularly cover nutrition, exercise, and stress relief as well as the latest medical advances. As of this writing, there are more than a handful of Web sites, including www.webMD.com and www.drkoop.com, the site of former surgeon general C. Everett Koop, offering virtual encyclopedias of medical information in plain English, and integrative medicine sites like the popular www.drweil.com. Of course, there is much of real value on these Web sites and in the publications mentioned here, but they pay their way with advertising, so bear that in mind while you surf, search, and research.

Antiaging Promises

Ponce de Leon failed in his quest to find the fountain of youth, but that hasn't quenched the desire to one-up the biological clock. The idea that we can tinker with the lifespan is hardly a modern obsession, although it often seems that way. *Makrobiotik*, a collection of diet and lifestyle recommendations published in 1787 by a German physician named Christopher Hufeland could be considered the first diet book. "The first serious attempt to develop a scientific prescription for longevity," according to a report on antiaging medicine from the International Longevity Center.

Despite the marketing hype that usually accompanies the latest weight-loss quick fix, one of the most promising "antiaging" interventions *is* about food, specifically a technique known as "calorie restriction." Well, you might be saying, most diets do that in one way or another. What is different about CR, as popularized in several books by Roy L. Walford, M.D., a UCLA pathologist and chief researcher of calorie restriction (see www.walford.com), is the emphasis on maintaining recommended daily allowances of essential nutrients while reducing calories far below the maintenance level. Such a regime would delay the onset of typical degenerative diseases of aging that occur between ages sixty and eighty. In his sixties, Dr. Walford was chosen as an "astronaut" in the Biosphere experiment.

At midlife and beyond, we get a clear message from our bodies that we don't need as many calories as younger folks. For whom are all those relaxed-fit jeans and chinos intended, after all? Our bodies are changing, "Yet nutrient needs stay the same or even increase," says Tufts University nutritionist Alice H. Lichtenstein, D.Sc., codeveloper of a modified food pyramid with Robert M. Russell, M.D., of the Jean Mayer USDA Human Nutrition Research Center on Aging at Tufts. As we get older, we need more antioxidants to build resistance against free-radical damage, Vitamin D and calcium to preserve strong bones, and folic acid to keep the brain functioning. The best way to get these nutrient-dense foods, say these experts, is from dark-colored vegetables and fruits packed with these essential vitamins, e.g., broccoli, spinach, and squashes in the vegetable category, and powerhouse fruits like blueberries, strawberries, and peaches.

As you probably suspect, most fast food and packaged snacks don't make the cut. Sorry, we can't have our cake and eat it, too. Calorie restriction, reports the International Longevity Center, "has clearly shown that it is possible to retard the rate of aging and extend . . . the life expectancy." It can extend life expectancy by 20 to 40 percent depending on your age when you begin the program. The twenty-five-year Okinawa Centenarian Study bears this out. So our mothers were right all along. Eat your vegetables!

Vitamin supplements remain controversial within the medical profession, particularly with regard to the efficacy of megadoses in maintaining health. The Living to 100 Web site, however, calls vitamin E "the best scientifically proven antioxidant" available, and noted that selenium has shown "dramatic effects in preventing cancer." Again, do your own research, including a talk with your doctor, before you decide to self-prescribe.

No matter what we do, the biological clock ticks for us all, and no one gets off this planet alive (except in a space suit for a short trip). Where we choose to put our attention now, whatever our age or physical condition, can make a significant contribution to how long and how well we live. Taking that to heart is one of the healthiest things we can do. "The question is not whether we will die, but how we will live," says Joan Borysenko, author (*Minding the Body, Mending the Mind* and others), psychologist and motivational speaker.

SHELF LIFE OR YOUR LIFE?

Bad news on trans fats, those innocent-sounding hydrogenated or partially hydrogenated fats so ubiquitous in packaged foods like stick margarine, breads, cookies, and snack foods. It's impossible to know how much of these fats you're eating because the labels aren't obliged to list that figure, so far. That may be changing. Food manufacturers hydrogenate fats to improve shelf life. The problem is that hydrogenated fats behave like saturated fats. Two recent Dutch studies linked trans fats to increased risks for heart disease. Most natural-food producers avoid using trans fats, and we'd like to see this adopted across the board.

Minding the Mind

Psychoneuroimmunology. It's a mouthful to say, but we expect to hear more about this emerging science in the future. It is an investigation of mind/body processes that may one day confirm what shamans and healers of every persuasion have been saying: The mind is a far more powerful tool in wellness than is currently accepted. We believe the so-called placebo effect—when people who think they are being given a particular drug respond to the treatment—is just one example of this amazing gift we share and by no means the most useful. It's easy to forget inborn healing power in an ethos that celebrates and rewards medical heroics, yet many doctors are leading the way. In his groundbreaking book *Healing Words*, Dr. Larry Dossey confirms the efficacy of a nonmedical intervention as old as human culture: the power of prayer to heal. As of this writing, New York University Medical Center was offering preoperative patients a workshop based on *Prepare for Surgery, Heal Faster: A Guide of Mind-Body Techniques* by Peggy Huddleston.

We are in no way suggesting that because the mind plays an important role in our wellness that we can think ourselves sick or cause a disease. Attitude may not be everything, but it counts. A 2002 study of 660 adults aged fifty and older from an Ohio community, published in the *Journal of Personality and Social Psychology*, found that people who had positive attitudes about aging lived more than seven years longer than those who didn't. It is also clear that lifestyle choices we freely make can either predispose us to, or protect us from, certain diseases. For example, we can choose to ignore the clear correlation between obesity and heart disease, diabetes, even some forms of cancer that become more of a threat after age fifty, or we can decide to do something about those extra pounds while they are still manageable. As the success of twelve-step programs show, all habits, healthy or not, begin in the head.

A program created by Dean Ornish, M.D., was the first to document that heart disease could be halted or even reversed by making better lifestyle choices. The Ornish program (described in his best-selling books) is founded on four pillars of wellness evident in studies on longevity: low-fat, whole-grain based diet; regular exercise (yoga is strongly recommended); stress management; and love and intimacy. Notice the strong holistic foundation. The program

is getting results: many participants are able to avoid surgery and
reduce or eliminate their medica-
tion. We believe the success of the
program depends less on its individual components, excellent as
they are, than in getting participants to make a commitment to
their own well-being.

Stress has become like the
weather: everyone complains about
it, but no one does anything about
it. Yet stress is something we create
in ourselves in reaction to external
events, and what we do, we can

> ### STRAIGHT FROM THE HEART
>
> According to a French study of 17,000 coronary deaths pub-lished in the journal *Heart*, men 25–54 are most vulnerable to heart attacks on Saturday and Sundays—possibly because that is when they exercise strenu-ously—as opposed to men fifty-five and older whose day of risk is Monday, when they confront the stress of work after a period of relaxation.

undo. We can learn to become less reactive, to turn off the stress—which always begins in the mind—before it turns up in our bodies in the form of compromised immunity and other ills. Meditation, visualization, breathwork (see Resources) are but a few of the proven techniques that trigger what Herbert Benson, M.D., has dubbed "the relaxation response" in his book of the same name. None is particularly esoteric, difficult to learn, or practice. All it takes is, well, making up your mind.

The Body Eclectic

Like it or not, around fifty we are squarely in use-it-or-lose-it terri-tory as regards physical fitness, including flexibility, strength, and endurance. If you've been an athlete of the armchair or weekend va-riety, throwing yourself into a hard workout invites problems, par-ticularly in the lower back, which bears the brunt of stress and our habits of sitting for long periods of time hunched over a PC. But there are at least three options that get the sedentary among us back into shape: tai chi, Pilates, and yoga.

All three have their own philosophy and forms, and much information is now available on each. Here's what these practices have in common that make them ideal for our age group:

1. They are available in gyms, health clubs, and studios, relatively easy to learn, fun to do, and noncompetitive. (Very important.)
2. Minimal equipment or special clothing required. (Traditionally, Pilates was performed on a specialized machine, but mat classes have since gained popularity.)
3. The intended effect of all three practices is holistic, i.e., they work on body, mind, and spirit.
4. Each stretches the muscles, moves and lubricates the joints, and improves circulation throughout the body.
5. Breathing is coordinated with movements. This encourages us to pay attention to the breath, and breathe more deeply, using more of our lung capacity.
6. Each is a low-impact exercise that relies on the body's own weight to strengthen bones and muscles.
7. Mental focus is enhanced.
8. All three are known to relieve stress and promote relaxation— one of the best forms of preventive medicine we know of.

Developed in China centuries ago, tai chi began as a form of martial arts. Today, it remains that country's exercise of choice. Visitors to Beijing often remark on the vitality of the gray-haired practitioners in public squares at sunrise, performing a series of graceful movements that resemble a slow-motion dance. In effect, the practitioner's own body moving through air provides all the weight and resistance necessary to tone muscles as well as improve circulation and balance. In addition to swimming, tai chi is often recommended as a safe, gentle exercise for people in recovery.

Pronounced pih-lah-teeze, Pilates is a series of movements that target the muscles of the abdomen, lower back, thighs, and buttocks, known to practitioners as the body's "core." The idea is that the core muscles in your back and pelvis help keep your spine properly aligned as you move, preventing injury and developing the lean, taut midsection characteristic of devoted practitioners. Developed by Joseph Pilates, a German gymnast who served as a nurse during World War I, the system originally relied on a collection of devices to help wounded soldiers regain their range of movement. When Pilates himself moved to New York, he began to apply his techniques to help dancers and athletes recover from injury. Many exercises are performed on modern versions of these original contraptions, but today most gyms teach mat Pilates and claim many of the same benefits.

As practicing yogis of a certain age (Marika also teaches yoga), we readily admit a bias toward this form of holistic health maintenance that works well for us. The long-lived vitality of yogi masters like centenarian T. Krishnamacharya and B.K.S. Iyengar, who still lectures and teaches in his eighties, is not lost on us. Postures, or asanas, are designed to take the body through a sequence of precise movements coordinated with the breath. Some schools favor a flowing, fast-paced routine guaranteed to make one sweat. Others encourage a slower, more meditative pace. In all cases, the idea is to "yoke" (the definition of yoga) mind, body, and breath (or spirit).

Howard's chronic back problems disappeared after he began his yoga practice nine years ago. Marika used yoga to reduce many of the symptoms of menopause and maintain bone density. Since we began taking lessons together, yoga has become part of our daily routine. We travel with our yoga mats—although even this minimal

SUPREME YOGA

Q: What do Justice Sandra Day O'Connor, Angelina Jolie, Tiger Woods, the New York Giants, and baseball star Orlando (El Duque) Hernandez have in common?
A: They all do yoga, says Bill Heavy, author of "A Life in Balance" (*Modern Maturity*, March/April 2002, see: http://www.modernmaturity.org/departments/2002/health/0310_health_a.html).

equipment is optional—and occasionally do standing postures in grocery checkout lines and in the aisles of airplanes.

Of course, any exercise carries some risk of injury and tai chi, Pilates, and yoga are no different. Consult a doctor before you begin any program, particularly if you've been exercising your right to skip exercise lately. Look for reputable teachers who can get you started in the right direction and minimize beginner frustration. Just remember we're all beginners at something or another. Books, tapes, and other teaching aids are great once you have mastered the basics, but they are no substitute for a teacher who can nip problems of potentially harmful posture or technique in the bud.

Mature Marathoners

Marathoners may be getting grayer, but they are giving their younger cohorts a run for their money. Consider the slim margins for the runners in a recent New York City marathon: the winners in the youngest group, Robert Quinn, age nineteen, at 2:56:15, and the winner of the 65–69 group, Manuel Rosales, age sixty-five, at 2:57:39. Similarly in the women's results, Anna Fyodorova, age nineteen, the leader in her group at 3:26:20, was beaten by Anna Thornhill, age sixty, at 3:25:39.

Maybe a marathon is not in your future, but mature marathoners have a lot to teach us about how to maintain, and even regain, health and vitality. The key to this, as to any form of exercise, is: choose what's enjoyable and start slowly. Tom Pontac, veteran of at least 125 marathons, got serious about running around his fortieth birthday and shows no signs of slowing down. Now in his sixties, he keeps a personal daily routine of 450 sit-ups, sixty pushups, and an hour of running. At Leisure World in Seal Beach, California, where he lives, Pontac founded Leisure Leggers, a running team with members between ages fifty-five and ninety. He coached the group of thirty for four months, preparing them to compete in the Long Beach Marathon. Not only has Pontac become the local guru on exercise and diet, he received *Runner's World* magazine's Golden Shoe award for his "contribution to the running community."

"Exercise makes you feel stronger and better," Pontac says. "It's never too late to get started. Almost anybody can change his or her lifestyle or life, beginning with regular walking." By the way, the motto of Leisure Leggers: "Growing old is not for sissies."

Family therapist and marathon racewalker Diane Wagger Wender discovered the sport in her sixties and was instantly hooked. She enrolled in a training program and before long, started to compete in local events. Then she decided to take a crack at the New York City Marathon and began training for the event, ten miles at first, then gradually increasing her range by two miles every other week. Under conditions even seasoned marathon athletes call severe—forty-six degrees and a stiff wind throughout—Wender completed the course in a respectable six hours and twenty-three minutes.

What did she learn from the experience? "A lot about myself, about motivation, about reinforcement. Of setting goals that are reachable, in small steps. That the training itself carries its own rewards." Wender now teaches racewalking.

Spirit

Some of us are free spirits. Some of us wear Easy Spirit sneakers. Spirit keeps turning up in sermons, graduation speeches, New Age titles, and advertising. Yet, because we can't see, hear, touch, taste, smell, or measure it, we have a hard time defining just what it is. Nonetheless, we know that spirit (or soul) is what lifts any life above a daily grind for survival, infuses it with joy, meaning, and purpose. Without spirit, our lives become dull, empty routines. There is no there, *there*. We humans have come up with ingenious ways to fill the void. But sex, drugs, and rock 'n' roll and their equivalents invite overindulgence and only work up to a point. Then, you are back where you started, maybe with a nasty hangover.

The good news is, spirit is like electricity: It's always present, available whenever we plug in and flip the switch. Think about the last time you felt yourself transported by a beautiful sunset or Beethoven's "Pastoral," or by gazing into the eyes of your beloved. Think about the so-called will to live that enables terminally ill people to extend their lives beyond expectations. Spirit pops up where it can, and we feel its effect psychologically and physiologically, even if we are skeptical about its existence.

We can choose to access spirit. And that is, by definition, an *inside* job even if it is performed out there. People of faith find spirit in prayer, rituals, singing of sacred songs, chanting, acts of generosity, and self-sacrifice. For artists, musicians, writers, and other creative types, spirit is the muse. To invite her in, they may read, listen to music, or take a long, solitary walk. For dedicated athletes, spirit is akin to flow—an altered state that enables them to perform effortlessly beyond their expectations. For committed yoga practitioners and meditators, connection to spirit is as near as the next mindful breath. It is a minimalist approach. Simple, but not necessarily easy. Physiologically, we understand this state as an endorphin rush, when we lose all sense of time, space, and distinction from our environment, and feel happy, safe, and whole. Spirit is what makes us human, so it is in our best interests to bring it to the surface regularly. Without spirit, we die.

Although everyone knows people who defy the canons of good health and live to a ripe old age, these are exceptions. For most of us, particularly at midlife and beyond, wellness—mind, body, and spirit—is no accident. It is based on choices we make every day. It is up to us to pay attention to the food we eat, the exercise we take, the people we associate with, and the thoughts we think. We must, to paraphrase poet Mary Oliver in "The Journey," be determined to save the only life we can save: our own.

Try This

Wellness is our natural state at any age. This is not only a spiritual concept, but a physical one that modern medicine, influenced by M.D.s like Herbert Benson, Deepak Chopra, and Andrew Weil, has begun to embrace. Whether or not you believe that our bodies are programmed to live for 120 years as some claim, it is well known that many of the so-called diseases of aging are the result of poor health habits established earlier in life. It's never too late to reclaim what is rightfully yours. Two caveats: 1. check with your own health-care provider before you try anything new and 2. don't expect overnight miracles. Use your notebook or journal to keep track of your progress, e.g., pounds lost; clothing that fits better; clearer eyes and skin; a better outlook on life; new friends; a sense that something is missing in your day if you don't walk, stop to smell the flowers, notice your breathing . . . you get the idea. That's when you know a healthy new habit has been adopted. Share your success with others. Maybe you'll start a trend.

STONE'S DAILY WELLNESS HABITS

- Do some gentle stretching before you begin your day, perhaps even while you are still in bed.

- After you brush your teeth, look at yourself in the mirror and smile. Feel silly? Good!

- Prepare a breakfast you like and eat it slowly, paying attention to the flavors and textures. You'll be less hungry later.

- Drink lots of water. Add fresh seasonal fruits and vegetables to your daily diet.

- Hug someone. Touch is good for you.

- Make requests and ask for help. Get comfortable with this idea.

- Read an inspirational text of your choice or some poetry.

- Treat yourself to flowers, in a garden or in the florist's window.

- Listen to music you enjoy. Focus on it completely.

- Take a moment to notice your breathing from time to time.

- Get rid of one item of clutter.

- Couch potato or weekend athlete, resolve to make exercise part of your daily routine. Here's an easy choice: find opportunities to walk whenever and wherever you can. You might even bump into someone interesting, and who knows where that could lead. Take the stairs.

- Make at least one day a week car-free. Walk, bike, take the train like our more enlightened European neighbors do. Good for you. Good for the planet.

- Choose an exercise you enjoy so you'll be motivated to keep doing it. Walking, swimming, tai chi, Pilates, or yoga are all wonderful ways to get your body in motion, especially if you've been a slacker about exercise. Start slowly and build up speed and endurance gradually. Don't get competitive, especially with yourself.

- Find a buddy to share your new found enthusiasm. You'll be surprised how much this adds to the fun, bolsters commitment, and improves your social and conversational skills.

- Celebrate the changes you notice, however small, with something that supports your healthy choices. New walking shoes, perhaps. A good quality yoga mat. A couple of hours at the botanical garden you've been meaning to visit.

- Join Weight Watchers or take a course in "conscious eating" (available at places like the Kripalu Center for Yoga and Health and Omega Institute). These all help you to slow down and enjoy what's on your plate. Your taste buds and digestive system will thank you.

- Experience a little mental feng shui: Think lovely thoughts. Adopt an attitude of gratitude. Seek out laughter every day.

- Slow down and pay attention to your moments. Be here now, said Ram Dass.

- Look into the eyes of the person you love until you find which eye is dominant, says yogi master Erich Schiffman. Then, beam in. Let your partner know you are really "seeing" him or her. Take turns.

- Seek a doctor who is interested in becoming a partner with you in your own wellness. Ask around and conduct your own interviews. Make a checklist of what's important to you, e.g., never having to wait naked in a chilly examination room tops our list.

- Create your own daily habits of wellness (see the Stones's own in sidebar for ideas). Turn your checklist into a good-looking poster and mount it on your wall.

Chapter 6.
Radical Departures

Travel is intensified living—maximum thrills per minute and one of the last great sources of legal adventure. Travel is freedom. It's recess, and we need it. —RICK STEVES,
Europe Through the Back Door

Travel is fatal to prejudice, bigotry and narrow-mindedness.
—SAMUEL CLEMENS (MARK TWAIN)

Everyday travelers are the planet's best ambassadors. Travel is humanity's greatest hope. —DON GEORGE,
GLOBAL TRAVEL EDITOR, LONELY PLANET

Since Jack Kerouac introduced his generation to life *On the Road*, travel has become the ultimate expression of individual freedom for all but the most intractable homebody. So it is no surprise that the urge to just take off tops the list of aspirations for those of us contemplating the end of—or recently released from—the nine-to-five routine. A trip is simultaneously a respite from routine and a reward even for hardcore, career road warriors like Howard, with thousands of free air miles burning a hole in his pocket and a sixth sense for good diners and customer-pleasing restaurants.

Once upon a time, travel was considered a necessary part of an educated person's life. The semester or junior year abroad spent becoming immersed in another language and culture was thought to be, well, *broadening*. Bargain airfares, jumbo jets, cookie-cutter hotels, and do-it-yourself Internet booking services make travel more accessible for more people. Lonely Planet sold more guide-books in the first eight months of 2002 than ever. But whether the popularity of travel can be said to have educated, enlightened, or helped create intercultural tolerance, is the question. Think about it: whom would you prefer to hang out with, a tourist or a traveler? Would you rather look at life as if it were a movie or museum exhibit, or dive in and experience it?

Whatever your preference, mass-market tourism, like its modern twin, consumerism, is the genie out of the bottle, the tooth-paste out of the tube. Inevitably, the size of our age group makes us a special target. Cruise lines in particular are banking on our lust to wander in comfort, convenience, and with minimal contact with native cultures. Gross tonnage has been on the rise steadily, with Cunard's forthcoming *Queen Mary II* topping out at 150,000 gross tons. Princess Cruises plans three new vessels for 2003–04 featur-ing "Discos suspended high above the stern. 72 percent outside cabins. 710 cabins have private balconies; 3 dining rooms, 2 atri-ums, 3 main showrooms, largest casino afloat; 5 pools, 9-hole put-ting green." For celebrities and wannabes with deeper pockets, exclusive island resorts tucked away in the Caribbean offer pam-pered getaways, accessible by private jet or water craft.

We enjoy creature comforts as much as anyone, but they don't have to be on the top of our list when we travel. The problem with a luxury cruise or exclusive resort is that it can insulate you from the experiences you travel for. It's that much harder to connect. We have to be very determined to allow the places we visit to "invade our in-ner spheres and impact our souls," says Janet Lührs, author of *The Simple Living Guide* and passionate world traveler. Fortunately for our endangered planet and its inhabitants—both visitors and the visited—now there is ecotourism, described by The International Ecotourism Society as "Responsible travel to natural areas that conserves the environment and sustains the well-being of local people." Just the good old do-unto-others rule, which needs no translation.

Today, there are as many reasons to travel as there are travelers, and possibly more ink is devoted to the subject than any other. So our intention is not to add to the stockpile of travel literature. Instead, we want to explore the timeless idea that travel, whether near or far, can be a force for good—connection, discovery, experimentation, and learning about what it means to be part of the human family. Consider

> ## GOOD GUIDES
>
> For a comprehensive travelogue, with tips on fares, accommodations, sights, and eats, we recommend Arthur Frommer's *Budget Travel 2002*. One of the most complete of its genre, it even includes spas and resorts with a spiritual inclination. Guides from Lonely Planet are excellent, as is its Web site, www.lonelyplanet.com. (Yes, it is still possible to travel on $15 a day in Lhasa, Tibet, for example: Dorm: $3., Food: $4; transport, etc.: $7.) Don't overlook popular online reservation services like cheaptickets.com, expedia.com, travelocity.com and Orbitz.com, not only for the best fares, but for a quick take on your prospective destination.

this your invitation to slow down, lighten the load, forego the frills, and blend in. Go off-road whenever the opportunity presents itself.

A take-only-pictures-leave-only-footprints ethos, we're happy to report, is alive and well. Rita Golden Gelman, author of *Tales of a Female Nomad: Living at Large in the World* (see also Chapter 1), has made it her life for over fifteen years. Gelman decided to limit her travel to the developing world—she lived in Bali for eight years—where an annual budget of $10,000 is ample. She travels light and keeps her options open: "I find that making very loose plans, the kind that allow for digressions, or just wandering with no plans at all, hoping to come across people, events, or just snippets of daily life, is my kind of travel. I am not drawn to the places that are recommended in guide books, where I have to stand in line to see finished products like paintings, sculptures, buildings, even concerts. I'd much rather see the process, the artist in his studio, the gamelon rehearsal where the players sit their kids on their laps as they hit the brass keys, the carver carving."

If you are seeking something more up close and personal than a suntan and duty-free shopping in exchange for hours strapped into an uncomfortable seat, you're not alone. There is a parallel universe of affordable, mind-expanding travel alternatives, including some that don't require a passport. One of the best "vacations" we ever took was right in our own backyard—New York City. We slept at home, and with the money we didn't spend on airfare and accommodations, we took Manhattan as if we were first-time visitors from another country. Try this out for yourself.

You might consider going inward at a reputable spiritual retreat center like Esalen Institute on California's Pacific Coast or Kripalu Center for Yoga and Health in the Berkshires of Massachusetts (our favorites—but there are others). You might explore traveling by train, both in the U.S. and in Europe—a back-to-the-future move we highly endorse. Trains are the preferred mode of travel for millions of Europeans, but it also has a devoted following in North America. If there is a better way to leave your car at home (a political statement worth making), spread out, eat, drink, and even work in comfort, and arrive at your destination in a great mood, please let us know.

Once you arrive at your destination, what would you give to find clean, comfortable accommodations in a real neighborhood with a kitchen, laundry, and an unparalleled opportunity to make new friends? Alternatives to the hotel/motel scene like caretaking, a radical idea in accommodations that has its own fans, newsletter (*The Caretaker Gazette*), and Web site (www.caretaker.org); home exchange, another live-like-a-local option; and a unique "untour" service we discovered, give you all that, for a fraction of the cost of city-based hotels or no money at all (home exchange and caretaking).

Inward Bound: Esalen, Omega, Kripalu

For us, there is no better way to refresh ourselves and recharge our batteries than to spend time close to nature, including an exploration of our own nature, mind, body, and spirit. Here are three centers dedicated to personal growth and transformation, generally regarded as among the best in the United States (necktie- and pantyhose-free zones, every one of them).

Founded in 1962 by human potential pioneers, George Leonard and Michael Murphy, **Esalen Institute** in Big Sur, California, surely ranks as one of the most beautiful places on earth, both for its pristine location on rocky cliffs overlooking the Pacific, and for the quality of its faculty and workshops. You can't fail to notice the exceptionally mellow, helpful, kindly staff. The food is fresh and delicious—Esalen grows most of its organic vegetables on its 120-acre site—with excellent alternatives for those with vegetarian or nondairy preferences. You need to be signed up for a workshop to go to Esalen, but for those lucky enough to live nearby, it is possible to buy just room and board on short notice should a workshop fail to fill to capacity. The fabled mineral baths—bathing suit optional—are back in service, and the famed massages in the open air with the sound of the surf make Esalen as close to Nirvana as possible. A bonus to our Esalen experience was the Money Maturity workshop with George Kinder (see Introduction)—a life-transforming experience. Whether your interest is in dance, relationship work, reiki, yoga, or the visual arts, to name a few, chances are the catalogue has something for you. An Esalen weekend runs about $485; a seven-day visit, $1,370. Work/study programs are also available.

An equally comprehensive catalogue of weekend and weeklong seminars is offered by **Omega Institute for Holistic Studies** headquartered in Rhinebeck, New York. Omega's main facility has the feeling of a campus and no-frills accommodations, including camping. The center also runs year-round programs at Rhinebeck in the warmer months, with winter retreats during January and February at Maho Bay, St. John's, U.S. Virgin Islands, and Costa Rica from February through the end of April. Double occupancy, meals, and eco-adventures are included in the price of $1,410 per person. Omega also sponsors conferences in major cities, like its yoga conference in New York. Recently, its catalog included Drawing on the Right Side of the Brain, based on Betty Edwards's book of the same title, and in Costa Rica, Capturing the Spirit of Yoga, led by Kripalu-trained Sudhakar Ken McRae and his wife, Kathleen Knipp (a member of Marika's graduating class at Kripalu Center for Yoga and Health in 1998).

Considered by many in the yoga community to be the best yoga-training school in the United States, **Kripalu Center for Yoga & Health** in Lenox, Massachusetts, also offers other holistic programs in a year-round schedule, as well as extensive health services, including various forms of massage therapy, reiki, and private yoga sessions by appointment. All programs are offered in the main building, which was once a Jesuit monastery. As you might expect, the basic accommodations are Spartan, but clean and comfortable. Upgraded rooms are also available. Yoga classes, including gentle, moderate, and "hot," are offered daily, along with

Kripalu DansKinetics® and a changing menu of experiential workshops and courses under the broad headings of Yoga and Meditation; Health and Healing; Self and Spirit; and Outdoors and Fitness. Warm-weather workshops might combine yoga with hiking, horseback riding, or golf. You could take a workshop on Painting from the Source with artist Aviva Gold, or learn how to Transform Stress with Kripalu scholar-in-residence/yoga teacher/massage therapist Ken Nelson, Ph.D. Kripalu also offers conferences like Psychotherapy and Spirituality, with a workshop led by prominent authors and teachers like Daniel Goleman (*Emotional Intelligence*) and Thomas Moore (*Care of the Soul*). A weekend workshop, with dorm accommodations, starts at $238 per person, and includes three, lavish, vegetarian meals. The body needs feeding, too.

Making Tracks

In a nation dominated by the automobile and highways, it's refreshing to be reminded that others have found better solutions for moving large numbers of warm bodies across great distances, efficiently, pleasantly, with lower environmental impact. We are speaking of the European rail system—a network of 160,000 miles linking seventeen countries—to which Europe's governments are about to add an additional 2,046 miles and introduce a new generation of trains that reach top speeds of 217 miles per hour.

At those speeds, and with terminals located in the heart of major cities, trains are beginning to draw travelers away from their autos—gasoline is $4 per gallon across Europe—and seriously challenge the airline industry. Paris to Marseille is now only three hours on an express line launched in 2001. Says Philippe Calavia of Air France, "Our real competition in the domestic market is not other airlines, but the train."

If you don't live in Europe, or Turkey, Morocco, Algeria, Tunisia, or the former Soviet Union (Commonwealth of Independent States), you are eligible for the amazing Eurail Pass. Beloved by backpacking students for decades, Eurail has a number of packages, including some with discounts for couples or two friends traveling together. Average cost for fifteen travel days to be used within a month is $486, and you can go anywhere within the system, with an array of schedule choices. Use your imagination. The Orient Express or Trans-Siberian Railway, anyone?

From the passenger's perspective, a quick, reliable connection and reasonable cost is just the beginning. Newer trains have such onboard amenities as Internet connections, video and DVD rentals, and children's play areas. No restrictions on cell phone or laptop use, and, of course, you can take a walk anytime you wish. Trust us. After experiencing the smooth ride and fine dining on France's TGV (Train à Grande Vitesse) from Paris to Lyons and back in the eighties, we have become big fans of this mode of travel. The Eurail Pass is, as its advertising says, unsurpassable.

Sadly, we do not enjoy visionary leadership on the subject of a viable railway system in the United States, no doubt a factor of aggressive lobbying in Congress by the automobile and airline industries. Plagued with financial problems, Amtrak perennially teeters on the brink of extinction, despite its billing as "the best and most affordable way to really see the United States and Canada" and an economical North America Rail Pass (peak season fare is $674 for travel within thirty days). "Travelers who want to see the West by passenger rail might want to take that picturesque trip soon," wrote *Denver Post*'s Jeffrey Leib. Once a busy center for passenger trains, Denver's Union Station was down to one Amtrak train a day in each direction on the California-Chicago route. On a brighter note, Congress agreed to give Amtrak $1.2 billion for fiscal year 2004.

(European government subsidies for the track alone come to $12 billion a year.)

We need a few more cheerleaders like Jim Loomis, whose book, *All Aboard! The Complete North American Train Travel Guide* covers just about everything you need to know about travel by train in North America. And possibly there is a lesson to be learned from the few bright spots in rail travel in the United States: commuter rail service. It is working, even in highway-haunted California. In May 2002, in the Los Angeles area, Metrolink made stops at fifty-one stations on seven routes covering 507 miles, serving 33,571 riders on the average weekday. According to the California Department of Transportation (CalTrans), Metrolink cuts 21,374 auto trips each day (that's a lot of smog reduction). On the other side of the continent, a light rail line is under construction on the New Jersey side of the Hudson River, one of the most congested areas in the country— a key element in the economic and social revitalization of areas like Jersey City and Bayonne.

Here's a thought: pack your hiking boots or bicycle on board, then burn some extra calories by hitting the road on your own power. Bicycling enthusiasts, Steve Spindler and John Boyle teamed up with the goal of using their bikes and public transit to get places. They share their ideas on their Web site, www.bike map.com.

FOOTLOOSE

The automobile is the symbol of freedom in our youth and remains the preferred way to travel for many. But sit in a few bumper-to-bumper lines, waiting to get into Yellowstone or another popular national park in peak season, for example, and you begin to appreciate something you take for granted: your feet.

One of the most appealing aspects of hiking is the limited amount of equipment needed (unless, of course, you're carrying overnight supplies). A good pair of hiking boots with ankle supports, dry socks, water, sunscreen for clearings, bug repellent for wooded areas, and the simple desire to move your body along a trail at a pace that satisfies you are about all you need. Freedom for you; minimal impact on the environment. Compare this to the gear of a typical golfer, skier, or scuba diver.

"Life is short; make time for adventure," is the motto of Hiker to Hiker, a not-for-profit organization founded and operated by Danielle (Danny) Bernstein. An avid hiker and member of the Appalachian Mountain Club (AMC) and Carolina Mountain Club, Bernstein has led day hikes, weekend trips, and long vacation trips for AMC. These include excursions to the Smokies, Shenandoah National Park in Virginia, Mt. Greylock in Massachussetts, and several trips to Colorado and the Canadian Rockies. The mission of Hiker to Hiker is to encourage the appreciation of wilderness areas and the diversity of people who use them. www.hikertohiker.org

Elder Trek (www.eldertrek.com/) bills itself as "the world's first adventure travel company designed exclusively for people fifty and over." With fifteen years of experience, the organization offers active, off-the-beaten-path, and small-group adventures in over fifty countries. All-inclusive land journeys focus on adventure, culture, and nature, e.g., a wildlife safari in Kenya; Mongolia by camel; hike to Patagonia's Torres del Paine, or the ruins of Angkor Wat, Cambodia.

See also Elderhostel, The Nature Conservancy, and the Sierra Club.

Homes Away from Home

Does the idea of living rent free in an extraordinary location in exchange for your services as a caretaker sound like an impossible dream?

Caretaking, as championed by Gary and Thea Dunn, former corporate fast-trackers and now owner/publishers of *The Caretaker Gazette*, is in a category of its own. It offers the adventurous and open-minded opportunities to sample a new location and self-sufficient lifestyle, and try out a new career as a property manager. Typically, free housing is offered in exchange for services that range from the garden variety of maintenance tasks to more sophisticated property management. Some caretaking gigs even include a salary and health insurance.

Global travelers themselves for twenty years, the Dunns chose to spend their time and resources in the developing world. What they learned changed their lives permanently: "With each subsequent trip, we became more aware of the contrasts between our lives in an affluent Connecticut suburb and life in the countries we visited in Africa and Asia. After ten years in the corporate world, we were in our early

---

WANTED

- **Caretaking couple** needed for a self-sufficient comfortable Alaska homestead. Whales, fish, caribou. Greenhouse, woodworking tools, loom, hot tub. Nature lovers and writers thrive here. Monthly stipend.

- **Guy/Gal Friday** for Caribbean property to help maintain house and gardens. Tranquil environment, mountain trails, pristine beaches. House including utilities in exchange for half-day Monday to Friday.

- **Artist's retreat** in the Ozark Mountains of northwest Arkansas, July through September.

Adapted from *The Caretaker Gazette*.

thirties and realized we were not content with the fast-paced, materialistic lifestyles of our colleagues and ourselves."

Inspired by the writings and teachings of Gandhi and the people they met around the world who live simply and contentedly, Gary and Thea quit the rat race to spend a year as volunteer teachers in India. Upon their return to the United States, the couple sought a home-based business and found in *The Caretaker Gazette* a way to share their simple-living philosophy with others. The circulation of the publication has grown from five hundred in 1993 when they purchased it to over seven thousand by 2001. In a recent edition of the sixteen-page newsletter, the property owners seeking qualified applicants outnumbered jobseekers roughly three to one. To subscribe, see www.caretaker.org or contact Gary Dunn at care taker@caretaker.org.

Home exchange, which became popular in the 1950s among the academic community, is an arrangement by which you live in someone else's home while they live in yours. Since accommodation expenses represent a significant part of any travel budget, the economic advantages need no explanation. Yet for ardent home exchangers, saving money is secondary to the other benefits. Despite accommodations that are modest relative to upscale resort hotels, proponents prefer home exchange for the off-the-beaten path locations, the extra space of an apartment or home, and the comfort and convenience of cooking and laundry facilities. All agree that reciprocity minimizes the worry of having strangers in your home. By the time arrangements are made, home exchangers have gotten to know each other through phone and e-mail. In fact, many have become friends over time.

Although the numbers remain modest, home exchange is growing 25 percent a year and over two million people are expected to be house-swapping by 2010, according to Helen Bergstein, founder and principal of www.digsville.com, a peer-to-peer, award-winning, home-exchange club, and an advocate of traveling the world the "home exchange way" since childhood, when she first experienced it. "No matter how well a travel book or guide describes a place, you can see it best from your 'own' backyard. When you are a guest in someone's home, you come away with a truer, richer experience. It's not unusual for a home exchanger to be personally escorted to the local market or be invited to attend a local event by a friendly neighbor. You can't get that experience on a tour or at a resort."

A number of quality home-exchange Web sites have come online in the last couple of years, which makes it simpler to find desirable opportunities almost anywhere in the world. For a small membership fee, you can post your own home listing, search the database of listings, and contact other members for the purpose of a home-exchange vacation, sabbatical, or extended stays. Digsville.com stands out from its competitors as the leading provider of home-exchange services for affinity groups, e.g., an alumni association or other networked group. It also offers the industry's only rating system for members to rate a recent exchange and partner. What Bergstein is aiming for is the creation of a sense of community among her members by providing them with password-protected message boards and other online support via e-mail and an 800 number.

Another option available with Digsville membership is hospitality or host exchange, in which you "host" visitors in your home, and in return, become their guest at some mutually agreeable time. Like home exchange, these arrangements are an opportunity to enjoy an insider's perspective and experience generally not available to those just passing through.

The brainchild of veteran globetrotter and humanitarian, Hal Taussig, **Idyll Untours** also advocates authenticity for its clients, whom it sets up in modest, clean, private apartments and homes in smaller, out-of-the-way towns and remote villages in Europe and Vietnam for two-week to two-month immersions. Hardly the stuff of four-color spreads in upscale travel magazines perhaps, but that's the whole idea. "We want [our clients] to be able to imagine that they've become residents of their chosen country for a short time, experiencing the life of the people rather than just sightseeing," says Taussig, a firm believer that "when people have contact with a way of life that is different from their own, they are much less willing to make war on other cultures."

Like Helen Bergstein's, Taussig's "aha!" came from personal experience as a part of the academic community. On a sabbatical tour of Europe, he discovered "how much more deeply rooted Europeans were in tradition and how that gave them a deeper sense of community than we have." Convinced that educators would benefit from a similar experience, Taussig wrote *Shoestring Sabbatical* on his return. The book drew enquiries from people looking to follow in his footsteps. In 1975, with a $5,000 loan from a friend, Idyll Untours was launched.

Changing minds one traveler at a time would be enough for most people, but social entrepreneur Taussig has a higher purpose for his business. He channels all the profits from his travel agency into the Idyll Development Foundation, which makes low-interest loans to projects that provide jobs and housing for the poor. Your travel dollars at work.

Way to go!

Try This

- Stay home #1. Take a vacation in your own city, town, or area. Approach it like a visitor, discover what you've been missing and save a bundle. Dorothy was right: There really is no place like home.

- Stay home #2. Pick a language that intrigues you and sign up for a language immersion course. Language (as we Americans have been slow to realize) is the key to another culture. Do it with a partner and make it a social event.

- Stay home #3. Spend several hours putting all those family photographs into an album or create a travel scrapbook. A memorable trip you can take in your slippers.

- Take minivacations that refresh and stretch you. Not those so-called long weekends during which you try to cram a week's worth of sightseeing into seventy-two hours, but an hour or two whenever the mood strikes you. Here are a few ideas to experiment with:

  > Visit a farmer's market, chat up the vendors and your neighbors. Ask for a recipe using the fresh produce and try it out right away.
  > Go apple picking with your grandchildren or special friends, then make a batch of apple crisp together. Bonding at its best.
  > Visit a museum on a subject you've never explored before, e.g., fly fishing (Livingston Manor, New York); opera (the Enrico Caruso Museum, Brooklyn); motorcycles (Sturgis, Mississippi). More at www.unusualmuseums.org/
  > Sit quietly in a public space—near a water fountain is ideal—and catch humans in the act of being human. People watching is just as fascinating in your town as on the Champs Elysées.

- Ask a friend with a passion—gardening, throwing clay pots, desktop design, sewing, baking bread, bird watching, chess, making cheese, you name it—to let you be an apprentice or student for half a day. Who knows? A whole new world could open up, not to mention the excitement of being a beginner at something.

- Host a student or family from another country in your home. A true win-win situation for all concerned. They get to experience how you live up close and personal. You experience their language, culture, and insights about your way of life. You get a whole new perspective on your hometown (and home). There are several organizations to check out, but a good place to begin is AFS (formerly American Field Service), a fifty-three-year old cultural exchange program, www.usa.afs.org/.

Chapter 7. Resources: Books, Web Sites, and Other Tools

At the start of this book, we invited you on a journey unlike any other you have taken before, an exploration of what the rest of your life is likely to be. Our insights were based on our own experiences and the wisdom of many other people. A selected list from our research appears on the list below and on www.2young2retire.com, the Web site of Retirement Alternatives. Consider the following books and online resources as trail markers for your own journey. And remember to pass along what you discover and learn to others who follow you. It's only fair.

General Reading

Cohen, Gene D., M.D., Ph.D. *The Creative Age: Awakening Human Potential in the Second Half of Life.* New York: HarperCollins, 2001.

Friedan, Betty. *Fountain of Age.* New York: Simon and Schuster, 1993. Will light your fire.

Roszak, Theodore. *America the Wise: The Longevity Revolution and True Wealth of Nations.* Boston and New York: Houghton Mifflin Company, 1998. Find out who you are and where you are going.

Chapter 1. Money: The Prose of Life

Books

Brock, Fred. *Retire on Less Than You Think.* New York: Henry Holt and Company, 2004. Discount the *R* word, but read this book for its straight talk on finances in later life. From the "Seniority" columnist of *The New York Times.*

DeGraaf, John, David Wann, and Thomas H. Haylor. *Affluenza: The All-Consuming Epidemic.* San Francisco: Berret-Koehler, 2001. Also a PBS special, available through www.pbs.org.

Dominguez, Joe and Vicki Robin. *Your Money or Your Life: Transforming Your Relationship with Money and Achieving Financial Independence.* New York: Penguin, 1992. Tough medicine, but you'll feel much better in the morning.

Gelman, Rita Golden. *Female Nomad: Living at Large in the World.* New York: Three Rivers Press, 2002. How little you can live on if you know where to live.

Hawken, Paul. *The Ecology of Commerce: A Declaration of Sustainability.* New York, Harper Business, 1994. Hope and optimism we can use.

Kinder, George. *Seven Stages of Money Maturity: Understanding the Spirit and Value of Money in Your Life.* New York: Dell/Random House, 1999.

Kingston, Karen. *Clear Your Clutter with Feng Shui.* New York: Broadway Books, 1998. Spiritual, life-changing.

Klainer, Pamela York. *How Much Is Enough: Harness the Power of Your Money Story—and Change Your Life.* New York: Basic Books, 2002.

Luhrs, Janet. *Simple Living Guide.* New York: Broadway Books, 1997. The bible of voluntary simplicity.

Phillips, Michael. *The Seven Laws of Money.* Boston: Shambhala Publications, 1974. Spiritually astute, this is a must-read for anyone who lives in a money economy.

Pollan, Stephen M. and Mark Levine. *Die Broke.* New York: Harper-Collins Publishers, 1997. A literary two-by-four upside the head on the subject.

Schor, Juliet B. *The Overspent American.* New York: Harper/Perennial, 1999. Not a pretty picture.

Sinetar, Marsha. *Do What You Love, the Money Will Follow.* New York: Bantam Doubleday, 1987. She doesn't say *how soon,* of course, but the principles are worth considering.

Wasik, John F. *Retire Early—and Live the Life You Want Now.* New York: Henry Holt, 1999. Despite the title and the apparent emphasis on money, Wasik's book is filled with gems of advice for the off-road thinker.

Web Sites and Other Tools

AARP Work and Career Study AARP & Roper September 2002, and a 1998 study: www.aarp.org.

Affluenza A PBS Special about the "all consuming epidemic" is available in VHS from www.pbs.org.

Center for a New American Dream Helping Americans consume responsibly to protect the environment, enhance quality of life, and promote social justice: www.newdream.org.

Co-op America Strategies for responsible investment, see: www.coopamerica.org/individual/personalfinance/investment/IP INTT03.HTM.

Hate Financial Planning? You're not the Lone Ranger. Created by ING Bank, www.ihatefinancialplanning.com has an excellent exercise called What's Your Money Personality?

Motley Fool Smart about many aspects of money, but surprisingly foolish about the inevitability of retirement. Nonetheless, worth a visit: www.fool.com.

Ruralburbia Small-town alternatives to urban sprawl, traffic jams, and a declining quality of life: www.ruralburbia.com.

Second Wind: Workers, Retirement, and Social Security From Rutgers University's Heldrich Center for Workforce Development: www.heldrich.rutgers.edu. Click on Work Trends.

Seven Stages of Money Maturity "There is another way of living with money": www.sevenstages.com.

Simple Living "Tools, examples & contacts for conscious, simple, healthy & restorative living": www.simpleliving.net.

Chapter 2. It's Not Working

Books

Bateson, Mary Catherine. *Composing a Life*. New York: Plume, 1990. Still fresh and important.

Berner, Jeff. *The Joy of Working from Home: Making a Life While Making a Living*. San Francisco: Berret-Koehler Publisher, 1994. Pithy, practical, and fun to read, from someone who has walked the walk. Berner is a 2young2retire.com columnist.

Bolles, Richard N. *What Color Is Your Parachute?* Berkeley, California: Ten Speed Press, 2002. The grandfather of career books, loaded with practical advice on where to look, what to do, and how to listen to your heart.

Cantor, Dorothy. *What Do You Want to Do When You Grow Up?* New York: Little Brown, 2001. The exercises deliver!

Goldberg, Beverly. *Age Works: What Corporate America Must Do to Survive the Graying of the Workforce.* New York: Free Press, 2000. Smart answers to the impending labor shortage.

Griffiths, Bob. *Do What You Love for the Rest of Your Life: A Practical Guide to Career Change and Personal Renewal.* New York: Ballantine Books, 2001. A personal story with much to offer career-changers.

Harkness, Helen. *Don't Stop the Career Clock: Rejecting the Myth of Aging for a New Way to Work in the 21st Century.* Palo Alto, California: Davies-Black, 1999. The author speaks nationally on the subject.

Hawken, Paul. *Growing a Business.* New York: Simon & Schuster, 1988. Wonderful ideas from the founder of Smith and Hawken. A personal favorite. Don't start a business without it!

Kersey, Cynthia. *Unstoppable: 45 Powerful Stories of Perseverance and Triumph from People Just Like You.* Naperville, Illinois: Sourcebooks, 1998. Down to earth yet uplifting.

Peters, Tom. *The Pursuit of Wow! Every Person's Guide to Topsy-Turvy Times.* New York: Vintage Book/Random House, 1994. Not your run-of-the-mill business book.

Pink, Daniel. *Free Agent Nation: The Future of Working for Yourself.* New York: Warner Books, 2002. Futuristic and fascinating, a new way to think about life and work in the twenty-first century.

Richardson, Cheryl. *Take Time for Your Life.* New York: Broadway Books, 1999. Accessible and rewarding. From one of the first life coaches to attain national prominence.

Sher, Barbara. *It's Only Too Late If You Don't Start Now: How to Create*

Your Second Life at Any Age. New York: Dell, 1998. Also see *Wishcraft.* Sher pulls no punches, bless her schoolmarm heart!

Toms, Michael and Justine Willis. *True Work: Doing What You Love and Loving What You Do.* New York: Bell Tower/Harmony Books/ Crown Publishers, 1998. An inspiring work from the founders of New Dimensions Radio.

Whyte, David. *The Heart Aroused: Poetry and the Preservation of Soul in Corporate America.* New York: Bantam, 1996. Whyte does the unimaginable: makes *Beowulf* a parable about work.

Web Sites and Other Tools

Write that business plan with help from bizplanit: www.bizplanit.com/vplan.htm.

From Dow Jones, a premier site for career changers: www.careerjournal.com.

Coryat Casting www.coryatcasting.com or contact Henry or Isabel Coryat directly at hicoryat@valstar.net.

Fun and inspiring, browse this site for ideas about your dream job: www.dreamjobstogo.com.

Dan Pink's useful site based on his book: www.freeagentnation.com.

Our favorite for its zippy articles. Perfect for the freelancer among you: www.guru.com.

Two places to post your resume: www.headhunter.net and www.seniorjobbank.com.

www.jobhuntersbible.com, created by Richard (*What Color Is Your Parachute?*) Bolles, and based on the same philosophy and principles as his revolutionary career book.

It's a monster, all right, but terrific for taking the pulse of business: www.monster.com.

As the name suggests, the National Business Incubation Association "provides entrepreneurs with the expertise, networks and tools they need to make their ventures successful": www.nbia.org.

For you "indies" out there: www.workingsolo.com.

Service Corps of Retired Executives (SCORE) offers valuable tips for any would-be entrepreneur, free of charge: www.score.org.

See True Stories about people just like you at 2young2retire.com, The Web Site of Retirement Alternatives: www.2young2retire.com.

Chapter 3. It Is Working: Volunteering Revisited

Books and Articles
Blaustein, Arthur I. *Make a Difference: Your Guide to Volunteering and Community Service.* Berkeley, California: Heyday Books, 2002.
Coplin, William D. *How You Can Help: An Easy Guide to Incorporating Good Deeds into Your Everyday Life.* New York: Routledge, 2000.
Dychtwald, Ken. *Age Wave: How the Most Important Trend of Our Time Will Change Our Future.* New York: Bantam Doubleday, 1990. Speaks and consults on the subject.

Freedman, Marc. *Prime Time: How the Baby Boomers Will Revolutionize Retirement and Transform America.* New York: PublicAffairs, Perseus Books Group, 1999. Passionate, full of inspiring role models.

Larned, Marianne, ed. *Stone Soup for the World: Life-Changing Stories of Kindness & Courageous Acts of Service.* New York: MJF Books, 1998. This is a good place to begin your exploration.

Lawson, Douglas. *101 Ways You Can Improve the World and Your Life.* La Jolla, California: Alti Publishing, 1998.

Mancuso, Anthony. *How to Form a Nonprofit Corporation, 4th Edition.* Berkeley, California: Nolo Press, 2001. A classic of the genre, it is packed with the relevant forms in print and on an attached CD. Don't start your nonprofit organization without it!

McAdams, Dan P. "Generativity: The New Definition of Success," in *Spirituality & Health,* fall 2001. www.spiritualityhealth.com/newsh/items/article/item_3566.html.

Roszak, Theodore. *America the Wise: The Longevity Revolution and True Wealth of Nations.* Boston and New York: Houghton Mifflin Company, 1998. Provocative and inspiring.

Schachter-Shalomi, Zalman. *From Age-ing to Sage-ing: A Profound New Vision of Growing Older.* New York: Warner Books, 1997.

Web Sites and Other Tools

Action Without Borders, www.idealist.org, is a "global network of individuals and organizations working to build a world where all people can live free and dignified lives." It has led many seekers to volunteer or paid positions at nonprofit organizations.

Big Brother/Big Sister, www.bbbsa.org, is one of the oldest of its kind. Connect with children who need the attention and support of caring adults.

CASA, an acronym for Court Appointed Special Advocate, is a national organization dedicated to homeless, abused, and neglected children. Find one in your area: www.nationalcasa.org.

Cross-Cultural Solutions provides opportunities to travel and volunteer with local nonprofit organizations in Eastern Europe, Asia, Africa, and Latin America. Short and long-term assignments are available: www.crossculturalsolutions.org.

Experience Corps® taps the experience of caring older adults in schools and youth-serving organizations to improve academic performance and development of young people: www.experience corps.org.

Global Exchange is a nonprofit research, education, and action center dedicated to promoting people-to-people ties around the world: www.globalexchange.org.

Global Volunteers (see www.2young2retire.com/goldberg.htm) coordinates teams of volunteers to work on short-term development projects in twenty countries: www.globalvolunteers.org.

Habitat for Humanity. If you have a hammer, muscle, and motivation, you can help needy families put a roof over their heads, in the United States and elsewhere. Jimmy and Rosalyn Carter do it: www.habitat.org.

Junior Achievement (www.ja.org/) enables business professionals to share their experience with students to show them what it takes to be successful. After all, kids are our future. Nationwide.

National Park Service. Exchange your volunteer hours for a hookup for your RV, perhaps, or enjoy interacting with other nature lovers in beautiful locations (see www.2young2retire.com/annmariah.html). Check the volunteer URL: http://www.nps.gov/volunteer/.

Peace Corps www.peacecorps.gov. See also www.2young2retire .com/lynnegarnet.htm.

Service Corps of Retired Executives (SCORE), where your experience in business helps people getting started on theirs. Part of the Small Business Administration: www.score.org.

Stand Up for Kids. A 99.5 percent volunteer-run, award-winning organization dedicated to the rescue of homeless and street children founded by Rick Koca, former naval officer. www.standup forkids.org.

Volunteer Match. The slogan says it all: Get out. Do good. www. volunteermatch.org/.

WorldTeach, a nonprofit, nongovernmental organization based at the Center for International Development at Harvard University, offers opportunities to live and work as volunteer teachers in developing countries: www.worldteach.org.

Chapter 4. 101 Opportunities for the Open-Minded

Books
Bolles, Richard N. *What Color Is Your Parachute?* Berkeley, California: Ten Speed Press, 2002. The grandfather of career books, loaded

with practical advice on where to look, what to do, and how to listen to your heart.

Cantor, Dorothy. *What Do You Want to Do When You Grow Up?* New York: Little Brown, 2001. Rewriting your autobiography.

Hawken, Paul. *Growing a Business.* New York: Simon & Schuster, 1988. A personal favorite. Don't start a business without it!

Kersey, Cynthia. *Unstoppable: 45 Powerful Stories of Perseverance and Triumph from People Just Like You.* Napier, Illinois: Sourcebooks, 1998. Belongs in your toolbox.

Nemko, Marty, and Sarah and Paul Edwards. *Cool Careers for Dummies®,* 2nd Edition. Foster City, California: IDG Books, 2001. Very cool.

Peters, Tom. *The Pursuit of Wow! Every Person's Guide to Topsy-Turvy Times.* New York: Vintage Book, Random House, 1994. From the author of the groundbreaking *In Search of Excellence,* a book that will make your entrepreneurial heart beat faster.

Pink, Daniel. *Free Agent Nation: The Future of Working for Yourself.* New York: Warner Books, 2002. Futuristic and fascinating.

Rogak, Lisa Angowski. *The Upstart Guide to Owning and Managing a Bed and Breakfast.* Upstart Publishing Co, 1994. Read it before you spend your life savings on that cute little inn.

Sher, Barbara. *It's Only Too Late If You Don't Start Now: How to Create Your Second Life at Any Age.* New York: Dell, 1998. Also see *Wishcraft.* Sher pulls no punches.

Toms, Michael and Justine Willis. *True Work: Doing What You Love and Loving What You Do.* New York:Bell Tower/Harmony Books/ Crown Publishers, Inc, 1998.

Web Sites and Other Tools

Adventure jobs: www.coolworks.com/olderbolder.htm.

Be cool. A sense of humor about the search for your next occupation is an important part of your toolkit. See www.working humor.com/cartoons.htm.

Computer-oriented free agents: www.guru.com.

Former Educators Wanted. PACE Program, Central Texas College, 6200 West Central Texas Expressway, P.O. Box 1800, Killeen, Texas 76540: www.ctcd.cc.tx.us. See also www.2young2retire. com/annmariah.html.

Job Quick Search: http://home.att.net/jobguide/. Check out the examples on the Web site before you plunk down $19.95 for the guide.

Part-time, seasonal, or temporary assignments. WorkRover. com posts thousands of hourly positions offered by reputable employers and matches your needs with theirs: www.workrover.com.

Working Today An association for independent contractors: www. workingtoday.org.

Chapter 5. Toward Wellness

Books

Benson, Herbert. *The Wellness Book: The Comprehensive Guide to Maintaining Health and Treating Stress-Related Illness.* New York: Fireside, 1993. From the author of the groundbreaking *The Relaxation Response.*

Borysenko, Joan. *Minding the Body, Mending the Mind.* New York: Bantam/Doubleday, 1993. A classic in the mind-body connection.

Cope, Stephen. *Yoga and the Quest for the True Self.* New York: Bantam Books, 1999. A spiritual journey from a gifted writer and yogi.

Dossey, Larry. *Healing Words: The Power of Prayer and the Practice of Medicine.* New York: Harper, 1997. The uses of prayer and other nonmedical intervention in healing.

Feuerstein, George and Larry Payne. *Yoga for Dummies.* Foster City, California: IDG Books, 1999. A "work-in, rather than a work-out," says coauthor Payne and an excellent place to start.

Herman, Ellie. *Pilates for Dummies.* New York: John Wiley & Sons, 2002.

Jahnke, Roger. *The Healing Promise of Qi: Creating Extraordinary Wellness Through Qigong and Tai Chi.* New York: Contemporary Books, 2000.

Kabat-Zinn, Jon. *Wherever You Go, There You Are.* New York: Hyperion, 1994. One of the best coaches for meditation practice.

Oliver, Mary. *New and Selected Poems.* Boston: Beacon Press, 1992. Simply powerful.

Ornish, Dean. *Eat More, Weigh Less: Dr. Dean Ornish's Life Choice Program for Losing Weight Safely While Eating Abundantly.* New York: Quill, 2000. Well-known approach to preventing and/or treating heart disease with diet, exercise, and stress-relieving practices including meditation and yoga. Recipes included.

Perls, Thomas T., et al. *Living to 100: Lessons in Living to Your Maximum Potential at Any Age.* Boston: Basic Books, 2000. Tips for your first century.

Sarno, John E. *Mind Over Back Pain.* Berkeley, California: Berkeley Pub Group, 1999. Sarno is one of the first to link muscular stress to one of the most chronic problems of our age. Life-altering for many back pain sufferers.

Schiffman, Erich. *Yoga: The Spirit and Practice of Moving into Stillness.* New York: Pocket Books, 1996. Yogi master Schiffman makes the ancient practice accessible for all. One of the best of its type. Instructions and photos.

University of California, Berkeley. "Stealth Fats: How Food Makers Hide Them from You," *Wellness Letter*, April 2002. www.well nessletter.com.

Walford, Roy L. *The Anti-Aging Plan*. New York: Four Walls, Eight Windows, 1994. Controversial, this calorie restriction regime claims to retard the aging process. It worked in laboratory animals.

Weil, Andrew. *Spontaneous Healing: How to Discover and Enhance Your Body's Natural Ability to Maintain and Heal Itself*. New York: Fawcett Columbine, 1995. Weil also puts out a popular newsletter.

Willcox, Bradley J., D. Craig Willcox, and Makoto Suzuki. *The Okinawa Program: Learn the Secrets to Healthy Longevity*. New York: Three Rivers Press, 2001. Based on the twenty-five-year Okinawa Centenarian study. Packed with great information.

Web Sites and Other Tools

Aging General information: www.agingresearch.org/healthtopics.cfm.

Andrew Weil: www.drweil.com.

Food Nutrition research from renowned source: www.hnrc.tufts. edu, includes a revised food pyramid.

Tai Chi Basic information: www.mtsu.edu/~jpurcell/Taichi/taichi. htm.

Vitamins Arguments in favor from The Healthy Foundation: www. healthfound.org.

Yoga Kripalu Center for Yoga and Health: www.kripalu.org. Find teachers, articles, yoga props: www.yogasite.com.

Chapter 6. Radical Departures

Books/Magazines

Barbour, Bill and Mary. *Home Exchange Vacationing: Your Guide to Free Accommodations*. Nashville, Tennessee: Rutledge Hill Press, 1996.

Bryson, Bill. *A Walk in the Woods: Rediscovering America on the Appalachian Trail*. New York: Broadway Books, 1999. Nobody does it better.

Frommer, Arthur, ed. *America on a Budget*. Special Annual Issue of Arthur Frommer's Budget Travel Magazine. (And other Frommer guides.)

Gelman, Rita Golden. *Tales of a Female Nomad: Living at Large in the World*. New York: Three Rivers Press, 2002. How little you can travel on if you know where to go.

Theroux, Paul. *The Old Patagonian Express*. Flat Rock, North Carolina: Mariner Books, 1997. Also *The Great Railway Bazaar* and *By Train Through the Americas*. Romancing the rails.

Check out Lonely Planet and Rough Guides for offbeat and off-the-beaten path guide books of high quality.

Web Sites and Other Tools

Amtrak basic information: www.amtrak.com/index.html. 1-800-USA-RAIL (872-7245).

Appalachian Mountain Club: www.outdoors.org/activities/index.shtml.

Back Roads (hiking organizers): www.backroads.com. 800-GO-ACTIVE (462-2848).

Caretaker Gazette: www.caretaker.org. Subscription newsletter.

Digsville, an online home-exchange community: www.digsville. com.

Ecotourism. The year 2002 was named the International Year of Ecotourism. www.ecotourism.org.

Elderhostel Adventures in Lifelong Learning® www.elderhostel. org for hiking and trips with an academic component.

ElderTrek Hiking for the fifty-plus: www.eldertrek.com.

Eurail basic information: www.eurail.com. To purchase tickets in the United States, check out these sites:

• New York City, CIT Tours, www.cit-tours.com.

• White Plains, New York, Rail Europe Group, www.raileurope.com.

• Rosemont, Illinois, DER Travel Services, www.dertravel.com.

Europe Through the Backdoor. Independent, economic, culturally broadening trips through Europe are the speciality of this site, headed by Rick Steves. www.ricksteves.com. E-mail rick@rick steves.com.

Hiker to Hiker: www.hikertohiker.org.

Home Exchange: www.homeexchange.com.

Idyll Untours: www.untours.com. Idyll Development Foundation, 1-888-868-6871.

Live Abroad, an organization dedicated to the expatriate lifestyle, see www.liveabroad.com.

National Park Service: www.nps.gov.

Ramblers Organization (British hiking group): www.ramblers.org.uk/index.html.

Sabbatical Home Exchange: www.sabbaticalhomes.com.

Sierra Club: www.sierraclub.org.

The Nature Conservancy "Saving the last great places on earth": www.nature.org.

Index